THE PRIME GRILL
COOKBOOK

THE PRIME GRILL COOKBOOK

REDEFINING THE KOSHER EXPERIENCE

DAVID KOLOTKIN and JOEY ALLAHAM

PELICAN PUBLISHING COMPANY

Gretna 2013

The word "Pelican" and the depiction of a pelican are
trademarks of Pelican Publishing Company, Inc., and are
registered in the U.S. Patent and Trademark Office.

ISBN: 9781455617302
E-book ISBN: 9781455617319

Printed in Singapore

Published by Pelican Publishing Company, Inc.
1000 Burmaster Street, Gretna, Louisiana 70053

We proudly dedicate this book to our loyal customers who have helped make our restaurant the shining success that it is today.

To our friends, our employees from the Prime Grill, and our families, all of whom made this book possible.

To my parents, Victor and Violet, my wife Lauren, and my children Victor, Violet, Jacob, Grace, and Maya . . . I love you with all my heart. To my mentor, Arthur Emil, for his guidance, friendship, and constant support.

—Joey Allaham, founder & owner

To my friends and family, namely my father Glen, sister Dawn, wife Jennifer, and most importantly to my mother Helene who has been suffering from Multiple Sclerosis for the past twenty years and has been a symbol of strength, wisdom, support, and guidance throughout my career.

—David Kolotkin, executive chef

Contents

Acknowledgments

To my entire kitchen crew who have been my backbone for the past decade at the Prime Grill—you know who you are.

To my current Chef De Cuisines Wilfredo Lopez and Chef Guillermo Quiroz, and my past Sous Chefs, Daniel Dorodo, Jared Lewin, and Servio Lopez.

To the Culinary Institute of America and Adriano Bokinac, who said yes, when everyone else said no.

To my friend and mentor, Michael Lomonaco.

To Shlomo Schwartz, for his endless hours recipe testing in the kitchen, and perhaps most importantly, Marissa Rosenberg for her tireless work toward making this book a reality.

Lastly, to my special partnership with the Prime Grill and its founder Joey Allaham.

Introduction

Over the last decade, the landscape of the kosher food and restaurant industry has experienced a seismic shift that has altered the entire experience of kosher fine dining. Once an under-saturated market filled with tired food and little tradition, "kosher" is now an industry filled with an abundance of quality, choice, and flavor.

The Prime Grill Cookbook will take you inside the restaurant that was at the forefront of the kosher culinary revolution in New York and around the world. With the opening of the Prime Grill in Midtown Manhattan, owner and founder Joey Allaham created the first high-end kosher steakhouse in New York City and in so doing, forever altered the public's perception of kosher food. The Prime Grill became a haven for the midtown power lunch crowd and the place where many successful and important business deals have been made. With a dining experience suitable for families, businessmen, ladies who lunch, and patrons looking for a relaxed, elegant atmosphere, the Prime Grill's menu offers delicious and inventive food appropriate for all types of occasions, which you will now be able to recreate in the comfort of your own kitchen.

This book will give readers an insider's look into the heart of the restaurant, accenting stories from its founder and chef with the recipes of the dishes that made the Prime Grill the crown jewel of kosher dining.

THE RESTAURANT

History

Joey Allaham was born in Damascus, Syria, on November 24, 1974. A fourth-generation butcher, Joey was destined to be a part of his family's multigenerational wholesale meat business. Fittingly, in Arabic, the name "Allaham" translates to "meat."

At a young age Joey began accompanying his grandfather to the slaughterhouse to learn about the business. At eight years old, Joey ate his first pieces of raw meat and started developing a palate for high-quality, delicious flavors. In 1991, as animosity towards the Syrian Jewish community continued to rise, the Allahams immigrated to the United States and settled in Brooklyn, New York. Though Joey had planned to follow a career in law, as his interest in the hospitality industry grew, he shifted his focus and returned to his family business of butchering and selling meat. He founded a wholesale business for various retailers, caterers, and individual clients in Brooklyn, New York.

Joey saw a gap in the market for a kosher steakhouse that could rival its non-kosher competitors and in 1999 began preparations for what would be the opening of his first restaurant, the Prime Grill. A resourceful businessman with no formal training in finance or the restaurant business, Joey found a partner, took out a loan, and only a year later, his dream was realized.

Prime was the obvious name choice, as the restaurant would focus on and serve only the highest-quality cuts of meat. In addition, Joey wanted the name to be simple. The best food that a man can put in his mouth is a simple piece of meat cooked to perfection with salt and pepper,

an axiom that Joey wanted to be represented in the name of the restaurant. Narrowing in on the location was the next task. Joey knew the importance of location and found the perfect storefront, located at 60 East 49th Street, just a stone's throw away from the business sector and featuring a large patio and the prospect of a busy lunch crowd. Arthur Emil, the prominent restaurateur and owner of Windows on the World, owned the lease at the Midtown Manhattan location. Prior to meeting Joey, Emil had two failed concepts in the location, and their introduction could not have come at a better time. With his natural charisma, Joey convinced Emil to open his kosher steakhouse. Emil would go on to be Joey's lifelong mentor and friend until his death in 2011.

Mark Markowitz was selected as the architect and construction began. In terms of design Joey envisioned creating a classic steakhouse that would age well with time—just like his simple but delicious cuts of meat. The color scheme was minimal, but sophisticated, and the place would have a warm inviting feeling.

With a conservative *New York Times* announcement and no advertising budget, the Prime Grill opened its doors with a surprisingly strong first quarter. Word of the restaurant spread on its own, with referrals helping to generate the bulk of the business. However, despite high aspirations and a moderately successful opening, business was not a joy ride at the outset. There were nights when the restaurant was empty and a year and a half into the business 9/11 hit New York City and the world changed. Despite the difficult times, Joey stuck to the path he carved out for himself. Every day he would train the butchers and oversee all aspects of the business from the front of the house to the back of the house. In the post-9/11 world, customers weren't spending as lavishly on extravagant dining experiences; morale was low. Joey knew that this would not be forever, but he had to give his customers a reason to pick up and move forward; he needed to push the envelope even further.

He went on a desperate search to find a new chef who could create a more invigorating menu. In late September 2001, about eighteen months after the Prime Grill opened for business, Chef David Kolotkin was hired to be the executive chef, and he has since led the kitchen for the past decade. Although not a formal partnership, Chef David and Joey have been a team in every sense, creating and perfecting the menu and overall dining experience.

From there, Joey put together a strong team of like-minded individuals who cared tremendously about food, dining, and taking pride in their craft. The majority of the people who work at the Prime Grill today have been with the company since its first days and continue to share in the mission Joey started thirteen years ago.

While writing this book, we closed up thirteen wonderful years in our founding location and moved northwest to 25 West 56th Street. In our new location, the Prime Grill continues to feature the classic favorites that our customers have always loved. However, we have used this opportunity to introduce a new generation of kosher cuisine including expanded menu options, a true wood-brick oven (a rarity), and more private dining capabilities. The new facility features bi-level seating for more than 360 diners and a special wine-themed private room with a premier collection of rare kosher wines. It was time to

make a move in early 2013, and the new Prime Grill is bigger and better than ever.

We feel fortunate to have hosted so many clients over the years, celebrating familial events, closing business deals, or just getting together with friends. There is nothing more gratifying and we look forward to our customers' support long into the future.

Joey Allaham, thirteen years old, at his Bar Mitzvah

THE PRIME GRILL COOKBOOK

Joey Allaham, in the Prime Grill's former dry aging room

Victor Allaham, father of Joey Allaham

The Prime Grill's former entrance, 60 East 49th Street

The former Bar at the Prime Grill location

The former Main Dining Room at the Prime Grill location

The Private Room at the former Prime Grill location

Sushi Bar Area at the former Prime Grill location

The Chef

I have wanted to be a chef for as long as I can remember. As a young child, I used to go with my family to Kutsher's Resort in Upstate New York and it was there that I developed a love for the hospitality industry. Though I consider myself a people person, comfortable in front of crowds and mingling with guests, I understood from early on that my true passion was food. Rather than resign myself to a front-of-house position, I chose to focus my career where my skills were best suited—in the kitchen, making delicious food.

Though the trips upstate piqued my interest in a career in the culinary world, it was perhaps the matriarchs of my family who instilled the passion. Growing up in Huntington, Long Island, my mother placed a high level of importance on family time around the dinner table, which we all looked forward to. Every evening we had a complete meal filled with fresh fish, the highest quality meats, and healthy vegetables and starches. Her passion for cooking and satisfying the palates of my sister and I instilled in me an appreciation for food and the dining experience that I have carried with me throughout my career.

My first cooking experience took place in my garage at twelve years old. At a time when most kids my age were playing baseball, I found myself more interested in making my own ice cream. During that summer, I would take the money I made from my landscaping job and ride my bike down Woodbury Road to the deli to buy heavy cream, sugar, and cinnamon. My dad helped me purchase an American Eagle ice cream machine and I would spend hours in the garage mixing and matching flavors to create the perfect ice cream.

My grandmother Bella was another food inspiration. As an immigrant from Poland, my grandma Bella became Americanized over the years, but she never lost her Polish accent or her talents in the kitchen. My family would spend many of the Jewish holidays at her home where she would make dishes from her native Poland, most memorably her Chicken Soup and Potted Chicken. Food is the language that brought my family together, and the common thread that continues to bring countless others together, which is something I truly value as a restaurant chef.

As a junior-high-school student with the dream of being a chef, I had the drive and the passion, but no experience, which, I learned early on, is everything in this industry. The first person who gave me a chance was Adriano Bokinac. After walking into every restaurant in the town near my home, I found myself in Adriano's restaurant on one of the busiest nights of the week. Adriano looked at me with a blank stare, walked away, and within two minutes returned with an apron and said, "follow me." That first night was the beginning of my career. I started as a pot washer in Villa Adriano and left a few years later as a cook. After high school, I enrolled in the Culinary Institute of America where I graduated in 1993 with the "Most Likely to Succeed Award." I was fortunate enough to complete my apprenticeship from the CIA at the world famous 21 Club in New York City under Chef Michael

Lomanaco, who later took me in to be his senior sous chef at Windows on the World and has since become a lifelong mentor and friend.

After 9/11, I had an internal awakening. I was ready to do something totally different and head in a new culinary direction, though I was unsure of what that might be. It's times like these where the most unexpected gifts can present themselves, and for me, it came in the form of a call from a headhunter.

The conversation, which I remember very clearly, went like this: "I have a great steakhouse for you, high volume, lots of meat, steaks, Steven Spielberg comes with his mom," to which I quickly responded, "So what's the catch?" The opportunity he was describing sounded too good to be true. His final remark was the kicker: "Well, it's kosher!"

I quickly flashed back to the days at Windows on the World when the kosher caterers would torch the kitchen with their heavy prep, and I remember not being impressed, especially because of the poor reputation of kosher food. After about three weeks of dodging the headhunter's phone calls, I finally decided to give the Prime Grill a try. I was out with some friends a few blocks away and went inside, took a seat at the bar, and ordered the house-made sausages. I was very skeptical that this "kosher" establishment was making its own sausages, and even more curious to see if they were tasty. While waiting, the bartender was trying to sell me a glass of wine, which I was also very skeptical about, having only previously experienced one kosher wine, Manischewitz. The bartender gave me a cabernet that was full of flavor and body and I loved it. I ordered a steak in addition to the sausages, and when they both arrived I was pleasantly surprised—the sausages had a lot of flavor and the steak was cooked perfectly. The restaurant was playing some hip music and had a great crowd all night. As I finished my meal I got really excited. I paid the bill, pulled out my StarTAC flip phone with the retractable antenna, got on

the phone with the headhunter, and said, "I would love to meet with Joey. I think I can do great things here."

I met with Joey, the visionary behind the business, and he shared with me his passion for meat and his drive to give people "the best of the best." I knew from that meeting that our passions aligned, and felt we could make a great team. From there, as they say, the rest is history.

Though my formal culinary training had no relevance in the kosher world, it was not something that I perceived as a weakness. From the outset, I felt it served as a strength knowing that I could bring something to the table that the Prime Grill customers had never experienced before. The Mashgiach (the first kosher term I encountered on the job), Chaim, became my sidekick and I learned all the don'ts of keeping kosher in my first weeks. He never taught me the do's—those I had to come up with on my own, but I learned fast.

In my first week, Joey asked me to run a special. Not knowing the sophistication of my clientele I put together something that I knew could not go wrong: a BBQ duck spring roll with my house-made BBQ sauce and duck confit. I made ten orders and Joey loved it. The next thing I knew he got on the phone and started calling all of his friends to come down to the restaurant to try the special. Within ten minutes I was sold out, so the next day I made twenty orders and the same thing happened. This occurred every day for the rest of that week, until Joey decided to add the dish to the menu. To this day the BBQ Duck Spring Rolls are one of my best-selling items on the menu.

I started at the Prime Grill on October 1, 2001 and have since opened the Prime Grill in Miami, Westhampton, two locations in New York City, Prime Butcher Baker, and Prime at the Bentley. In addition, I have consulted for Joey on a number of projects and I also oversee the kitchen at Solo. As I am finishing this book and reflecting on my career, I am overwhelmed with emotion as we close a chapter in the Prime Grill story. As we move from our original and founding location at 60 East 49th Street a few blocks north to 25 West 56th Street, I look forward to recreating the new Prime Grill and elevating it to a higher level. Most importantly, I look forward to creating new memories and new dishes in our new home. With this book I am excited to bring the Prime Grill into your home.

—Chef David Kolotkin

The Kitchen

The Prime Grill is a Glatt Kosher meat and pareve kitchen. Though the kosher kitchen is quite different than the non-kosher kitchen, at their most fundamental levels, the foundations are the same. The primary differences are the separate stations for all of our meat and fish items, and our entire restaurant is dairy free. Most importantly, all of the ingredients are certified Glatt Kosher, and we have a kosher supervisor known as a Mashgiach present in the restaurant during all operating hours. The Mashgiach is the first person who comes into the restaurant each day and the last person to leave. He is, in fact, the only person who has the keys to the lifelines of the kitchen, and he opens and locks each part of our kitchen every day, including all of the walk-ins, ovens, and dry storage rooms. The Mashgiach's life's work is to know all of the aspects of kosher and implement that knowledge into the restaurant. "Kosher" is not only a difference between products, but it is a lifestyle. Kosher food is defined as food that is fit for consumption based on Jewish law as decreed in the bible. The Mashgiach ensures that the customer truly is getting a kosher meal. His responsibilities range from receiving all products to washing vegetables to lighting the fire on the stove each day. Chaim Maryles was the first Mashgiach that the Prime Grill employed and he still works at the restaurant to this day. Our restaurant has two Mashgichim at all times: one upstairs watching the front of the house and the line and the second one downstairs in the prep kitchen washing the vegetables and overseeing receivables and butchers.

A successful restaurant must be organized. Our kitchen was designed as an open kitchen, which faces out to our bar. Many restaurants like to hide what goes on in their kitchens, but at the Prime Grill we like to invite our customers into the experience with us. This gives a feeling that the customer is part of the cooking process.

To understand our kitchen is to know where everything is. Right in the center you will find the grill station. We have two brothers working on the grill who have been working at the Prime Grill since before Chef David Kolotkin took over as executive chef. The grill takes on 65 percent of the business and the brothers work together as if they are one. The rumor in our kitchen is that the brothers don't even like each other, but during an entire service period they are silent and act as one unit and never show any hard feelings. In fact they support each other and work quickly and efficiently.

To the left of the grill is our sauté and roast station. The ducks and chickens are roasted here and the spring rolls are cooked until crisp. The lead line cook on this station acts as a liaison between the grill and the expediter, who is the last person to see the plate before it leaves the kitchen.

Moving all the way to the right side of the kitchen, we have our fish station. The fish station, as mentioned earlier, is kept completely separate from the meat station. At the fish station, all of the fish is butchered and portioned by the lead fish cook, who also sautés and plates the fish components for each dish.

To the far left of the grill you will find our fry and

soup du jour station. Our fry station is completely pareve, which means that no product cooked there contains meat or dairy.

The salad station, which is typically an entry-level station for a beginner cook, is actually our second-heaviest station in the kitchen. This station contains a lot of composite salads that require an organized, attentive, and well-prepared cook.

Next is the sushi station, located to the right of the bar, overlooking the dining room. Chef Makoto Kemayama, our executive chef at Prime KO, created and developed the sushi program at the Prime Grill. Our current sushi chef, Ridwan "Wibi" Wibisono, executes this station with two assistants.

The final station is our pastry station. Chef Felencia Darius is the corporate pastry chef for the Prime group of restaurants. Chef Felencia's talent speaks for itself—she is constantly pushing the envelope and creating dairy-free desserts that are both delicious and beautiful.

Downstairs you will find a prep kitchen, butcher department, dry aging room, dry storage, and all of our walk-ins where we keep fresh produce. This is the heart and soul of the kitchen, where all of the foundations are created. Stocks, soups, duck confit, and our famous BBQ sauce are all prepped and cooked downstairs before the restaurant opens each day.

The butcher room is led by our head butcher, Tereso Sanchez, and assisted by his brother Mauro and four other butcher assistants. Trained by Joey and his father, Victor Allaham, the butchers receive all of the meat from the Mashgiach and check it for quality, marbleization, and, perhaps most importantly, to ensure that it is "prime." Once all of the meat is properly checked, the butchers prepare the meat for aging by trimming pieces on the band saw and placing the meat in the dry aging box for a minimum of twenty-one days. Tereso has trained his team to be very organized so that all of the meats are labeled properly and maintained in the dry aging room at the proper temperature. The butchers also prepare all of the charcuterie, and they marinate and portion all of the meats for our various locations.

The chef de cuisine, Wilfredo Lopez, assists the chef in executing all of the daily tasks of his staff. The chefs meet weekly to discuss the menu items and fine tune dishes that are and are not selling. The menus at the Prime Grill feature four changes throughout the year—two major and two smaller alterations to focus on seasonal ingredients. The staples always remain the same, but we have fun with novelty items, such as roast duck, roasted chicken plate, composite salads, and soups. Chef "Willy," who serves as Chef David's right-hand man, is an especially integral part of the menu development process.

Our head steward is the lifeline of our restaurant. Ramon Solano began his career at the Prime Grill on the first day that it opened. Ramon aids in all of the receivables and upkeep of the restaurants. While the Masghiach is checking for Kashrut, Ramon is checking for quality. In addition to rotating stock and managing the porters, he also maintains the overall cleanliness and repairs of the restaurant. In this business when you find someone that you truly trust and can rely on, you hold on to them. Ramon is one of those people, and though he is not Jewish, he knows an exorbitant amount of information and values what we do as a kosher establishment.

Executive Chef David Kolotkin and Chef Wilfredo Lopez

Chet Wilfredo Lopez

Salad Station

Grill Station

Sushi Station

Mashgiach Meir Tabibi

Both Mashgiach's: (left to right) Meir Tabibi and Chaim Maryles

Head Steward Ramon Solano

The Dry Aging Room and Charcuterie

Our dry aging techniques are one of the most integral processes that sets the Prime Grill apart from the competition. As the pioneers in this field amongst the kosher market, the Allahams passed down their methods and taught the Prime Grill butcher staff how to accurately perform this process. The operation of dry aging is most simply described as a reaction that causes the fibers to break down, tenderizing the meat from the outside in. Dry aged meat is considerably more flavorful, because as the moisture dissipates, the contents become more concentrated. The steaks are placed in a dark dry aging room set at 37-39 degrees, with fans blowing to keep the air moving. We dry age our meats for a minimum of twenty-one days, and on special occasions we have a sixty-day age selection.

Since opening, the Prime Grill has always made its own fresh sausage and fresh beef jerky. In 2002, Chef David Kolotkin introduced a duck prosciutto and a duck bresaola. In the years since, we have also expanded the menu to include an entire charcuterie plate consisting of pepperoni, salami, and pâté, which is all made in-house.

Head Butcher Tereso Sanchez, far left, and his team

The Dry Aging Room

Lunch

Appetizers

Grilled Wagyu Angus Ribs
red cabbage slaw & asian marinade

House Smoked Wild Organic King Salmon
grilled asparagus, poached egg, crispy shallots & truffle oil

Boston Lettuce With Beefsteak Tomatoes
toasted sunflower seeds, sliced vidalia onions beef fry & creamy jalapeno ranch dressing

The Prime Grill Salad
crisp romaine, red & yellow tomatoes, cucumbers, garlic croutons & onions tossed in a citrus-cumin vinaigrette

Bresaola Carpaccio
cured beef filet, arugula, roasted peppers, toasted pine nuts, shiitake chips, crispy onions & reduced port-wine drizzle

Classic Caesar Salad
crisp romaine hearts, garlic croutons, creamy anchovy & garlic dressing

Atlantic Salmon Tartar
horseradish, capers, avocado & yucca chips

Soups

Soup du Jour
freshly made daily

Grandma Bella's Chicken Noodle Soup
traditional warm chicken broth with a mélange of seasonal vegetables

Silky Corn Bisque
spicy popcorn garnish

Charcuterie Kitchen

Charcuterie Board
bresaola, salami, spicy sausage & veal pate
served with cornichons, hot pickled cherry peppers,
whole grain french mustard & toasted baguette

House Made Loukaniko Greek Sausage
gigante bean & tomato stew, mint salad

PG Signature Beef Jerky
our traditional house-smoked beef jerky

Sandwiches
all sandwiches served with french fries

Our Original 14oz Prime Burger
toasted bun with classic garnishes

BBQ Short Rib Sandwich
pulled bbq'd beef, crispy onions topped with avocado

The Master's Burger
special dry-aged black angus grind
served with classic garnishes & french fries

Grilled Chicken Breast Sandwich
romaine, sliced tomatoes, crispy onions, pickles, avocado, ranch dressing served on a brioche bun

Filet Steak Sandwich
roasted peppers, onions & mushrooms
served with a creamy horseradish sauce

BLT Sandwich
enhanced beef, lettuce, tomato
with lemon aioli on toasted white bread

Smokehouse Burger
smoked 14oz "sirloin" burger, grilled pastrami,
house sauce & classic garnishes

"Fish & Chips " Sandwich
new england battered cod, tartar sauce, sweet gherkins,
lettuce, tomato & onions on a toasted bun

Wild King Salmon Burger
topped with radish sprouts, cucumber noodles & dill cream

Moroccan Lamb Burger
served with a dollop of mint "yogurt"

Lunch
Entrées
Entrée Salads

Chimichurri Salad
argentinean spiced diced meat, chopped mesclun, tomato, corn,
avocado, black beans, onions & chimichurri vinaigrette

with your choice of:
Grilled Organic Chicken Breast
Prime Angus Filet

Cobb Salad
shredded romaine hearts, avocado, diced tomatoes & onions,
sliced egg in a creamy horseradish basil dressing

with your choice of:
Grilled Organic Chicken Breast
Grilled Wild Salmon Filet
Sliced Prime Angus Filet

Grilled Chicken Paillard
arugula, calamata olives, roasted tomatoes, shaved fennel,
caramelized onions & red wine oregano vinaigrette

Chicken Chopped Salad
romaine, tomatoes, avocado, tobacco onions, egg, roasted beets,
beef fry & ranch dressing

Pepper Crusted Tuna Niçoise
seared sashimi quality tuna steak served over mixed greens, egg,
tomatoes, haricot verte, caper berries
& niçoise olives tossed in a tomato vinaigrette

Asian Style Duck Salad
cold stir fried noodles, cabbage, bean sprouts, enoki mushrooms,
baby corn, sesame, wonton chips & a sweet soy glaze

Entrées

Market Fish
composed daily

Potato Wrapped King Salmon
sautéed okra, tomatoes, corn, jalapeno peppers & horseradish sauce

"Everything" Crusted Sushi Grade Tuna
chickpea puree & bagel crostini

Pasta of The Day
prepared daily

Smoked BBQ Short Ribs
sautéed broccolini, pickled cherry peppers & garlic,
hush puppies

12oz Dry-Aged Beef Tips
served with house-made french fries

Pan Roasted Chilean Sea Bass
curried cauliflower puree, enoki mushrooms, baby bok choy & teriyaki sauce

USDA PRIME
Steaks
From Our Private Dry Aging Room
served with béarnaise & red wine shallot sauce

all steaks served with french fries & an oven-roasted tomato

Petite 8oz "Filet"	Buffalo Chopped Steak	Center Cut 14oz Rib Eye*
Prime Grill 10oz "Filet"	Prime Reserve Cut 10oz	Pepper Crusted 10oz "Filet"
Garlic & Herb Crusted Prime Grill 12oz	Petite Reserve Cut 5oz	Prime New York 21oz Rib
"Filet"	Chimichurri Marinated Hangar 8oz Steak	Lamb Chops

All Natural Prime Certified Black Angus Beef
Hand Selected From Our Butcher Shop "BB PRIME"
served with french fries & an oven roasted tomato, béarnaise & red wine shallot sauce

8oz "Filet"	14oz Rib Eye	8oz Reserve Cut

Sides

Sautéed Garlic Spinach	House-Made French Fries	Grilled Market Vegetables
Creamed Organic Spinach	Seasoned Texas Fries	Sautéed Mushrooms & Onions
Creamy Whipped Yukon Gold Potatoes	Roasted Artichokes	

Dinner

Appetizers

Crackling Duck Salad
warm duck confit & cracklings, arugula, frisee, tomato,
red onion, poached egg & champagne vinaigrette

Grilled Wagyu Angus Ribs
red cabbage slaw & asian marinade

Crispy Veal Sweetbreads & Tongue Duet
sweet & sour cabbage stir-fry, white bean puree
& cider-vinegar essence

House-Smoked Wild Organic King Salmon
grilled asparagus, poached egg, crispy shallots & truffle oil

Classic Beef Tartar
served over beef carpaccio with citrus-caper vinaigrette,
sun dried tomato & pistachio baked crostini

BBQ Duck Spring Rolls
house dipping sauce

Bowfin Caviar
honey-jalapeno-corn blini, parve crème fraiche,
chopped chives & mimosa of egg

Atlantic Salmon Tartar
horseradish, capers, avocado & yucca chips

Maryland-Style Fish Cake
whole grain mustard veloute, black bean & corn salsa

Slider Bar

all sliders served with shoe-string potatoes

Kobe Beef Sliders
pickled chips & ketchup

Buffalo Chicken Sliders
fresh herbs & spicy bbq sauce

Moroccan Lamb Sliders
arugula & mint yogurt

Brisket Sliders
whole grain mustard aioli

Porcini & Black Angus Sliders
wild mushrooms & porcini aioli

Assortment of Sliders
one of each

Charcuterie Kitchen

Charcuterie Board
bresaola, salami, spicy sausage & veal pate
served with cornichons, hot pickled cherry peppers,
whole grain french mustard & toasted baguette

Pate Du Jour
petite greens, onion marmalade & toast

House Made Loukaniko Greek Sausage
gigante bean & tomato stew, mint salad

PG Signature Beef Jerky
our traditional house-smoked beef jerky

Soups

Soup Du Jour
freshly made daily

Grandma Bella's Chicken Noodle Soup
traditional warm chicken broth
with a mélange of seasonal vegetables

Silky Corn Bisque
spicy popcorn garnish

Salads

Prime Grill Salad
crisp romaine topped with red & yellow tomatoes, cucumbers, garlic
croutons & onions tossed in a citrus-cumin vinaigrette

Classic Caesar Salad
crisp romaine hearts, garlic croutons, creamy anchovy
& garlic dressing

Bresaola Carpaccio
cured beef filet, arugula, roasted peppers, toasted pine nuts, shiitake
chips, crispy onions & reduced port-wine drizzle

Boston Lettuce With Beefsteak Tomatoes
toasted sunflower seeds, sliced vidalia onions, beef fry & creamy
jalapeno ranch dressing

Chicken Chopped Salad
romaine, tomatoes, avocado, tobacco onions,
egg, roasted beets, beef fry & ranch dressing

Dinner

Entrees

"Everything" Crusted Sushi Grade Tuna
chickpea puree & bagel crostini

Vegetable & Polenta Terrine
asparagus, zucchini, yellow squash & charred tomato coulis (vegan)

Potato Wrapped King Salmon
sautéed okra, tomatoes, corn, jalapeno peppers
& horseradish sauce

Pan Roasted Chilean Sea Bass
curried cauliflower puree, enoki mushrooms,
baby bok choy & teriyaki sauce

Porcini Burger
the original prime burger with roasted porcini mushrooms,
porcini aioli & steak fries

Lemon & Rosemary Rotisserie Chicken
½ chicken, sausage stuffing, cranberry relish,
haricot vert almondine & pan gravy

12oz Dry-Aged Beef Tips
served with tobacco onions

Smoked BBQ Short Ribs
sautéed broccolini, pickled cherry peppers & garlic,
hush puppies

Long Island Breast of Duck
spicy sausage, chestnuts, swiss chard,
quinoa & duck confit, pomegranate syrup

Wood Grilled 16oz Veal Chop
sweet potato puree, braised kale, local apple & onion compote
& whole grain mustard sauce

Mustard & Rosemary Crusted Rack of Lamb
eggplant & mushroom purée, fava beans
& lamb glace

The Master's Burger
special dry-aged black angus grind
served with classic garnishes & french fries

USDA PRIME

Steaks
From Our In-House Dry Aging Room
served with béarnaise & red wine shallot sauce

Petite 8oz "Filet"
Prime Grill 10oz "Filet"
Garlic & Herb Crusted 12oz Prime
Grill "Filet"
Center Cut 14oz Rib Eye

Prime New York 21oz Rib
Park Avenue 20oz Rib Eye
Chimichurri Marinated 8oz Hanger
Prime Reserve Cut 10oz
Petite Reserve Cut 5oz

Pepper Crusted 10oz "Filet"
Black Angus 18oz Filet
Texas Style 14oz Rib Eye

All Natural Prime Certified Black Angus Beef
Hand Selected From Our Butcher Shop "BB PRIME"
served with béarnaise & red wine shallot sauce

| 8oz "Filet" | 14oz Rib Eye | 8oz Reserve Cut |

USDA PRIME

Daily Specials
Sunday - Prime Grill "T" Bone Steak
Monday – Tender Sliced Sirloin Strip Steak
Tuesday - Delmonico Steak
Wednesday - Roasted Prime Rib
Thursday - Black Angus Beef

Sides

Roasted Artichokes
with sun-dried tomatoes, apricots

Steak Fries drizzled in Truffle Oil

Grilled Jumbo Asparagus

Fully Loaded Potato Skins
with beef chili, parve cheese, "sour cream,"
scallions

Sautéed Garlic Spinach
Sautéed Onions & Mushrooms
Crispy Zucchini Sticks

Garlic Bread
Creamy Whipped
Yukon Gold Potatoes
Creamed Organic Spinach
Seasoned Texas Fries
French Fries

Sushi Bar

Appetizers

Edamame
steamed green soy beans

Tuna Tartar Truffle
tuna tartar, avocado, tostada chips with truffle oil
& teriyaki sauce

Sushi Petite
tuna, salmon, yellowtail & spicy tuna

Sashimi Salad
tuna, yellowtail, salmon & ginger dressing

Yellowtail "Carpaccio"
with yuzu ponzu & jalapeno, togarashi

Tuna Aburi
yellowfin lean tuna, bluefin fatty tuna, enoki, spicy miso,
ponzu sauce & garlic chips

Crispy Rice With Spicy Tuna
sweet jalapeno aioli sauce

Crispy Rice With Cooked Salmon
sweet jalapeno aioli sauce

Crispy Rice With Guacamole
avocado, sweet jalapeno ailoi

Prime Specials

Dragon Roll
salmon, tuna, cucumber inside & wrapped with
avocado

Seared Spicy Tuna Roll
tuna, cucumber topped with seared spicy tuna
& teriyaki sauce

Seared Salmon Mousse Roll
enoki mushrooms, string beans, asparagus,
tempura flakes & ginger-teriyaki sauce

Vegetable Guacamole Roll
carrot, string bean, avocado & ginger-teriyaki sauce

Salmon Spider Roll
avocado, carrot, string bean, fried onions &
tobiko

Katsumaki Roll
avocado, mock crab, sun dried tomatoes,
salmon, teriyaki & truffle oil,
lightly fried

Prime Grill Roll
grilled yuzu-miso glazed black cod,
cucumber, sesame-teriyaki sauce, topped
with tuna & avocado

Fire Dragon Roll
spicy tuna, wrapped with avocado

Cooked Spicy Tuna Roll
avocado, mock crab, cucumber
& spicy teriyaki sauce

Kyoto Roll
tuna, salmon, avocado, mango inside
& wrapped with soy paper (no rice)

Spa-Tuna Avocado Roll
spicy tuna wrapped with avocado (no rice)

Osaka Roll
spicy tuna & avocado topped with spicy salmon

Seared BBQ Salmon Roll
tuna, avocado & fried onions with bbq sauce
& teriyaki sauce

Park Avenue Roll
spicy salmon, cucumber & crunchy tempura
flakes rolled in soy paper topped with tuna,
salmon & yellowtail

Sushi & Sashimi

(Sashimi 2 Pieces)
seasonal availability

Lean Tuna
Fatty Tuna   MP
Spicy Tuna
Ikura

Yellowtail
Atlantic Salmon
Organic Irish Salmon

Sockeye Salmon*
Smoked Salmon
Striped Bass
All Natural Trout*

Sushi Rolls

inside out (rice outside) 8 pieces

Lean Tuna
Smoked Salmon
Fatty Tuna   MP
Salmon Skin Cucumber
Spicy Tuna

Salmon Avocado
Tuna Avocado
Yellowtail Scallion
Tuna Mango
Yellowtail Jalapeno

California
Spicy Yellowtail Miso
Vegetable
(choice of cucumber, avocado, asparagus,
carrot, string bean or spinach)

Entrées

Sashimi Platter
2 tuna, 2 yellowtail, 2 whitefish, 2 salmon, spicy tuna

Sushi Platter
2 tuna, 2 salmon, 2 yellowtail, 1 whitefish, cucumber avocado roll

Prime Platter
Sushi: tuna, yellowtail, salmon, whitefish, spicy tuna roll
Sashimi: tuna, yellowtail, salmon, whitefish

Executive Sushi Platter
3 tuna, 2 yellowtail, 3 salmon, 2 whitefish, spicy tuna roll

All Well-Done Sushi Platter
crispy rice & cooked tuna with a spicy-sweet chili sauce,
cooked salmon avocado futomaki roll, fried california roll
topped with cooked salmon mousse

Desserts

Chocolate Caramel Dome
dark chocolate mousse, whiskey &
caramel mousse, pain d'espices

Tropical Vacherin
mango & coconut sorbet, pineapple compote
& salty macadamias

Chocolate Passion Fruit Pavé
flourless sponge & passion fruit anglaise

Molten Chocolate Cake
vanilla ice cream

Honey & Rosemary Apple Galette
rosemary infused honey, savory dough,
"buttered" pecan ice cream

Cookie Plate
assortment of home made cookies

Slice of Cake
Choice of Chocolate Fudge, Toasted Coconut Cake,
Tiramisu or Walnut Carrot Cake

Selection of Ice Creams & Sorbets

Drink Menu

Single Malts

Ardbeg 10yr
Arran 14yr Cask Strength
Arran Bourbon Cask
Balvenie 14yr Caribbean
Balvenie 15yr
Balvenie 17yr Peated Cask
Bowmore 12yr
Cragganmore 12yr
Dalmore 12yr
Dalmore Gran Reserve
Glenfiddich 12yr
Glenlivet 12yr
Glenmorangie 10yr
Glenmorangie 18yr
Glenrothes 1987 21yr
Glenrothes Reserve NV
Lagavulin 16yr
Laphroaig 10yr
Lombard 1991 13yr
Oban 14yr
Oban 1996 Distiller's Ed.
Talisker 10yr
Tomintoul 16yr
Tomintoul 27yr

Digestif

Amaretto Disaronno
Askalon Arak
Boukha Fig Brandy
Frangelico
Slivovitz Plum Brandy 10yr

Scotch & Whiskey

Buchanan's 18yr
Bushmills
Chivas 12yr
Chivas 18yr
Crown Royal
Jack Daniel's
Jameson
Johnny Walker Black
Johnny Walker Blue
Johnny Walker Gold
Kellan's

Bourbon

Basil Hayden
Booker's
Knob Creek
Maker's 46
Maker's Mark
Wild Turkey
Woodford Reserve

Tequila

Avión Silver
Los Arrangos Reposado
Patron Añejo
Patron Silver

Cognac

Louis Royer VS
Louis Royer VSOP
Louis Royer XO

Martinis

Crushed Q Margarita
Herradura Tequila
Muddled Cucumber
Orange Liqueur, Fresh Lime

Kiwi Martini
Absolut Vodka, Kiwi Purée
Triplesec, Fresh Lime
Splash Lemon-Lime Soda

Tropic Breeze
Stoli Vodka, Bombay Gin
Mango & Passion Purées
Triplesec

Electric Orange
Absolut Orange & Raspberry
Raspberry & Blood Orange
Purées, Splash OJ

Cool Blue
Ultimat Vodka
Orange Liqueur, Fresh Lime
Blueberry & Mango Purées

Mellow Yellow
Bacardi Rum, Peach Schnapps
Mango Purée, Pineapple
Splash Orange

Pear Martini
Absolut Pear & Vanilla
Splash Lemon-Lime Soda
Fresh Lime

Wild Cherry Cosmo
Stoli Wild Cherry
Triplesec, Fresh Lime
Splash Cranberry

Razzberry Truffle
Stoli Chocolate Razberi
Frangelico, Raspberry Purée
Crème de Cacao, Lemon

Cocktails and Sparklers

Mojitos
Classic, Blueberry, Mango
Strawberry, Raspberry
Cucumber, Passion

Daquiris
Bacardi Rum, Fresh Fruit
Citrus Liqueur
& a Splash of Lime

Martinis
Cosmopolitan
Manhattan
Sour Apple
Lemon Drop
Strawberry Passion
Chocolate
Espresso
Pomegranate
Lychee

Sparklers
Madras, Bellini
Blood Orange
Kir Royale, Mimosa

Margaritas
Classic, Golden, Mango
Strawberry, Raspberry
Passion

Cocktail
Sidecar
Whiskey Sour
Bloody Mary
Long Island Iced Tea
Amaretto Sour
Bay Breeze
Sea Breeze
Mint Julep
. . . and many more

Wines By The Glass

Whites

Baron Herzog Chardonnay, Central Coast, California, 2011
Dalton Safsufa Sauvignon-Viognier, Galilee, Israel, 2011
Borgo Reale Pinot Grigio, Delle Venezie, Italy, 2011
Hagafen Sauvignon Blanc, Napa Valley, California, 2011

Sparkling & Rose

Borgo Reale Prosecco, Veneto, Italy, NV
Borgo Reale Moscato D'Asti, Piedmont, Italy, 2010
Herzog Selection Rose' Brut, France, NV
Baron Herzog White Zinfandel, Oxnard, California, 2011

Reds

Binyamina Cabernet, Galilee, Israel, 2010
Kinneret Merlot, Samson, Israel, 2010
Segal's "Fusion" Cabernet-Merlot Blend, Galilee, Israel, 2011
Elvi Clasico Tempranillo, Ribera del Júcar, Spain 2010
Borgo Reale, Toscano Rosso, Tuscany, Italy, 2007
Chateau De Cor Bugeaud, Bordeaux, France 2010
Teal Lake Shiraz, South Eastern, Australia, 2011
Goose Bay Pinot Noir, East Coast, New Zealand, 2010
Herzog Reserve Cabernet, Alexander Valley, California, 2009

Wines By The Bottle

Champagne & Sparkling Wine

Borgo Reale Asti, Piedmont, Italy, NV
Rashi Pinot Brut, Piedmont, Italy, NV
Beckett's Flat Champenoise, Australia, NV
Drappier Champagne Carte Blanche Brut, France, NV
Drappier Champagne Carte d'Or, France, NV

White Wines

Herzog Reserve Chardonnay, Russian River, California, 2010
Baron Herzog Late Harvest Riesling, Monterrey, California, 2010
Goose Bay Sauvignon Blanc, South Island, New Zealand, 2011
Goose Bay Viognier, East Coast, New Zealand, 2009
Dalton Canaan White, Upper Galilee, Israel, 2011
Teperberg Collage, Chardonnay-Semillon, Samson, 2011

Region

Red Wines

Australia

Teal Lake Cabernet-Merlot, South Eastern, 2009
Beckett's Flat Five Stones Reserve Cabernet Sauvignon, 2008
Beckett's Flat Five Stones Shiraz, Margaret River, 2010

Italy

Borgo Reale Primitivo, Salento, 2008
Borgo Reale Maturo, Salento, 2010
Borgo Reale Pinot Noir, Puglia, 2011
Borgo Reale Chianti Reserva, Tuscany, 2008
Borgo Reale Brunello Di Montalcino, Tuscany, 2005

Israel

Barkan Pinotage, Samson, 2010
Segal's Special Reserve Cabernet, Galilee Heights, 2009
Binyamina Carignan, Galilee, 2010
Binyamina Reserve Cabernet, Galilee, 2009
Binyamina Reserve Shiraz, Galilee, 2009
Dalton Canaan Red, Galilee, 2011
Dalton Safsufa Cabernet Sauvignon, Galilee 2010
Dalton Safsufa Merlot, Galilee 2010
Kinneret Vintners Select, Samson, Israel, 2009
Shiloh Legend Reserve Blend, Judean Hills, 2009
Shiloh Shor Barbera, Judean Hills, 2009
Teperberg Silver Shiraz, Samson, 2009
Teperberg Terra Cabernet-Merlot, Judean Hills, 2010
The Cave Cabernet-Merlot Blend, Galilee, 2007

United States

Baron Herzog Merlot, Central Coast, 2010
Baron Herzog Syrah, Oxnard, 2008
Hagafen Merlot, Napa Valley, 2009
Hagafen Cabernet Sauvignon, Napa Valley, 2008
Hagafen Pinot Noir, Napa Valley, 2011
Hagafen Zinfandel, Napa Valley, 2006
Herzog Reserve Blend Cabernet-Zinfandel-Syrah, California, 2009
Herzog Reserve Cabernet, Napa Valley, 2009
Herzog Special Edition Cabernet Sauvignon, Chalk Hill, 2009

France

Cuvée du Centenaire Côtes du Rhône, NV
Chateau le Petit Chaban, Bordeaux, 2010
Chateau de Parsac, Montagne St. Emillion, 2011
Chateau Thénac Fleur du Périgord, Bergerac, 2010
Barons de Rothschild, Medoc, 2007
Chateau Rollan De By, Medoc, 2010
Chateau Tour Seran, Medoc, 2010
Chateau Haut Condissas Le Cadet, Medoc, 2003
Chateau Mareil, Medoc, 2004

Operations

Known to have one of the highest failure rates, the restaurant business requires hard work and perseverance. Profits only begin to show after the four to five year mark, and in many cases it might take even longer. Kosher restaurants also must get past a number of operational hurdles, which makes financing and sustaining a viable kosher restaurant even more impressive.

Among the many permits and licenses that one needs to operate a restaurant, our most important certificate is the kosher seal of approval, which we obtain from the Orthodox Union—the most prestigious of kosher certifications. The organization provides us with our Mashgichim, who watch over the restaurant and ensure the purification of our establishment. In addition to the physical kosher obligations, our restaurant also abides by Jewish Orthodox Law and closes on the Sabbath and a handful of Jewish holidays that do not permit work. Bearing in mind all of these closures, a kosher restaurant can end up operating anywhere from 200 to 250 days a year in total, whereas most other restaurant are open for business 365 days a year. In order to pay rent, salaries, and vendors, kosher establishments must work twice as hard to stay in business, which explains one of the many reasons your bill might be a little higher than at most other non-kosher restaurants.

Standards of cleanliness have increased throughout the restaurant industry in recent years (for the better) because of the health department's renewed dedication to keeping restaurants sanitary and their patrons in good health.

At the Prime Grill, we have increased our training and instituted weekly spot checks in which we go through the line and perform practice runs to make sure all food temperatures are correct and are outside the danger zone at either below 40 degrees or above 140 degrees.

The daily schedule begins each morning before the sun rises. The porters and opening Mashgiach arrive at the restaurant between 5:00 A.M. and 6:00 A.M. to prep for the day's schedule. At around 9:00 A.M., the back of house (BOH) arrives and starts setting up its food stations, followed by the front of house (FOH) employees and managers who all arrive between 10:00 A.M. and 10:30 A.M.

The restaurant opens Monday through Friday for lunch from 12:00 P.M. to 2:30 P.M. and then closes until we open for dinner Monday through Thursday from 5:30 P.M. to 10:30 P.M. The restaurant is closed on Friday evenings and re-opens for service one and a half hours after sundown on Saturday nights in the fall and winter seasons only. Sunday evenings the restaurant opens one hour earlier at 4:30 P.M.

The floor is run by our general manager, Inez Kincaid, and supported by our beverage director and floor manager, Danny Reina; second-floor manager, Tarik Gahdouani; and maitre d', Abdellatif Zegrani, better known to our loyal customers as "Ziggy."

A pre-meal meeting takes place before every service period begins. This meeting gives the managers a chance to evaluate service changes, specials on the menu, highlight guest and VIP's special requests, as well as review any issues from the night before that must be adjusted. In addition, the kitchen meets once a week to discuss sanitation, cleanliness, organization, and plate presentation.

Prior to the hustle of a service period, the FOH and BOH employees eat together every day at 11:15 A.M. and 4:15 P.M. for "family meal." Generally the prep cooks prepare the family meal, but oftentimes when we have people with different backgrounds working at the restaurant we give them an opportunity to cook some of their favorite dishes from their countries. The employees take a lot of pride in this and are very proud to show their heritage.

Dining is not just about the food. A patron will base his overall *experience* on a number of factors, namely the way in which he was greeted, friendliness of the staff, service, ambiance, décor, and the feeling he gets when he walks out the door. All of those factors are key ingredients to a successful dining experience and they all have to be spot on, at all times. This responsibility lies on our management team and they work very hard to train the staff and provide the best service possible to our guests.

To better serve our guests' needs we have expanded our beverage program to include a list of reputable kosher wines found throughout the world. This program is implemented by our beverage director, Danny Reina, and supported greatly by our strong relationship with the Royal Wine family. In addition, we have added a stronger cocktail menu and enhanced our beer selection.

Our restaurant team has a second set of hands offsite supporting the restaurant. Internally we have three key team members including a director of operations, Steven Traube; a marketing and public relations director, Marissa Rosenberg; and a banquet and events manager, Meital Bunker.

"Ziggy," maitre d'

RECIPES

Hors D'Oeuvres

During lunchtime, patrons can often find Joey sitting at the bar observing the dining room. While there, he frequently signals over to Chef David or one of the managers to share his observations, which at times can be very impulsive.

One day, Joey sat at the bar filling his mouth with handfuls of nuts. After two or three mouthfuls, he called Chef David over and said, "We can't keep serving a mixed nut selection at the bar. We need to give our patrons something that we make in-house and will be distinct to our bar. Can you come up with something?" Chef David agreed, and coincidentally he had been toying with a crisp potato chip. He thought that despite it being labeled a "cheap" item, a gourmet chip would make for a great "nosh" food at the bar if done in an upscale way. He replied, "I think I have something." The next day, rosemary potato chips appeared at the bar and instantly became a hit.

Prime Grill Rosemary Potato Chips

Serves: 1 heaping bowl

Special Equipment:
mandoline
spider strainer

3 medium-large russet potatoes, from Idaho
    preferred
Oil for frying
3-5 sprigs rosemary
1 tbsp. salt

Clean the potatoes, and with a mandoline slice them razor thin with the skin on. Place the slices of potato in a bath of cold water for at least 10 minutes. Drain the potatoes and set aside. In a saucepot, prepare the oil for frying. Heat oil to 375 degrees; use a fry thermometer as hot oil can be very dangerous. Fry the whole rosemary sprigs until crispy and golden. Remove the rosemary from the oil with a spider strainer and place onto a paper towel to drain excess oil. On a clean and dry surface, chop the crispy rosemary. Place the chopped rosemary in a small bowl, add 1 tablespoon of salt, and mix well. Working in handful-sized batches, fry the potatoes (in the same oil used to crisp the rosemary) for 1-3 minutes or until bubbles stop coming to the surface and the potatoes are golden brown. Remove and place on paper towels to absorb excess oil. Continue to fry remaining potato slices, one handful at a time. Season immediately with the rosemary salt and serve.

Chef's Tip: *Don't "over pack" when frying—this will ensure even cooking.*

Potato Bites with Roasted-Red-Pepper Aioli

Serves: 6-8

Special Equipment:
Pastry bag or disposable pastry bag

Potato Bites
2 large potatoes, russets from Idaho preferred
¼ cup sliced chives
½ cup pareve cream cheese
¼ cup crispy chopped beef fry
1 tbsp. margarine
¼ tsp. salt
⅛ tsp. pepper
Pinch nutmeg, freshly grated preferred
1 cup flour
3 eggs, beaten
1 quart ground panko
Oil for frying
See page 198 for Roasted-Red-Pepper Aioli recipe

Preheat the oven to 425 degrees and bake potatoes for 45 minutes to one hour or until fork tender. Let the potatoes cool and scoop out the insides. Combine potato in a mixing bowl with chives, cream cheese, cooked beef fry, margarine, salt, pepper, and nutmeg. Place mixture into a pastry bag, pipe long cylinders on a baking sheet (the length of the whole sheet), and place into the freezer for 10 minutes. Remove and cut into one-and-a-half-inch bite-size cylinders. Dredge each cylinder in the flour, then the egg, and then the ground panko. In a medium-to-large sauté pan heat the oil to 375 degrees—use a fry thermometer as hot oil can be very dangerous—and fry until golden brown. Serve with the roasted red pepper aioli for dipping.

Truffled Deviled Eggs

Serves: 4-6
Yields: 12 Canapés

Special Equipment:
Pastry bag or disposable pastry bag

6 eggs
1½ cups mayonnaise
1 tbsp. truffle oil
Pinch of white pepper
2½ tbsp. black truffle peelings, chopped
½ bunch chives, chopped
Sprinkle of sweet paprika

Place eggs in a pot of cold water, bring to a boil, and let simmer for 12 minutes. Drain the water, remove the eggs, and let cool. Peel the eggs and rinse under cold water. Slice the eggs in half lengthwise and remove the yolks from the egg whites and set aside. In a separate mixing bowl, mash the egg yolks and add the mayonnaise, truffle oil, white pepper, and truffle peelings. Whip in the food processor until fluffy. Place the mixture into a pastry bag and pipe gently into the egg whites. Garnish with a sprinkle of chives and sweet paprika.

Chef's Tip: These are usually served cold, but if you take them out of the refrigerator before serving for 20 minutes and serve at room temperature, the flavors will be more pronounced.

Crispy Eggplant Spring Rolls

Serves: 10-12

1 medium-sized eggplant

4 tbsp. extra-light olive oil

1 tsp. salt

⅛ tsp. ground white pepper

1 tbsp. garlic, minced

½ cup onion, minced

1 cup white button mushrooms, thinly sliced

⅛ tsp. cumin

1 tsp. paprika

¼ tsp. cayenne pepper

⅛ tsp. ground cardamom

1 fresh tomato, julienned

1 package (25 pieces) spring roll wrappers (Golden
   Bowl brand suggested)

Vegetable oil to fry

Preheat the oven to 350 degrees. Coat eggplant with extra-light olive oil and season with salt and white pepper. Wrap the eggplant tightly with aluminum foil and bake for 45 minutes to one hour until soft. Let the eggplant cool and remove the skin. In a sauté pan, sweat the garlic and onions until soft and translucent. Add the mushrooms and cook for two minutes. Add the cumin, paprika, cayenne pepper, and cardamom. When the fragrance starts to build from the dry spices, add the eggplant. Continue cooking on low-to-medium heat for 40 minutes, constantly moving the ingredients around to cook evenly. The mixture should be the consistency of a dry mashed potato. Cool the mixture in the refrigerator, place 1-1½ teaspoons of the mixture into each wrapper, and "envelope" wrap to create the spring rolls. In a small saucepot, add half-an-inch of vegetable oil and heat to 375 degrees. Deep-fry the spring rolls until golden brown for about 2 minutes on all sides.

Chef's Tip: To make an "envelope" fold, first fold in the sides, then bring the bottom up over the filling and seal with top "flap."

Corn and Honey Blini's Topped with Bowfin Caviar

It took twelve years to find a kosher caviar that I felt stood up to traditional caviar. True caviar comes from sturgeon and sturgeon only. Unfortunately, sturgeon does not have scales and therefore is a non kosher fish. The caviar that we are using comes from bowfin, which is a kosher fish with tremendous quality and flavor. It was always a dream of mine to create one of my favorite canapés and once I found this product I knew I could do it.

Serves: 4-6

¾ cup all purpose flour
½ cup yellow corn flour
1½ tsp. baking powder
½ tsp. kosher salt
1 egg
1 tbsp. honey
¾ cup non-dairy creamer (milk if serving dairy)
Vegetable oil to pan fry (3-5 tbsp.)
½ cup pareve sour cream
3 oz. bowfin caviar
½ cup mimosa of eggs
½ cup chopped chives

In a mixing bowl combine the flour, corn flour, baking powder, and salt. In a separate mixing bowl mix the egg, honey, and creamer until fully combined. Add the wet ingredients to the dry and stir until there are no lumps. Let the batter rest in the refrigerator for 5-10 minutes. Heat oil in a large skillet over medium heat and spoon batter into mini blini pancakes, the size of quarters (a teaspoon works well for this). When bubbles form on the top or when the blini are golden brown on the edges, flip and cook on the opposite side for 15 seconds. Spoon sour cream and a dollop of caviar on each blini, and garnish with the egg mimosa and chives on the side.

Chef's Tip: Serve warm for a contrast in temperatures and flavors.

Sweet and Spicy Cod

Serves: 4

Sweet Chili Sauce
1 tbsp. red chili flakes
1 tbsp. + 1 tsp. ketchup
1 tsp. paprika
1 cup sugar
1 cup water
3 tbsp. vinegar
Slurry mixture (1 tbsp. + 1 tsp. cornstarch with 2 tbsp.
   water)

Fried Cod
½ cup cornstarch
¾ cup flour (½ cup to combine with dry ingredients,
   ¼ cup for dredging)
1 tsp. baking powder
1 tsp. salt
¾ cup water
1 lb. cod or any delicate white fish, cut into 1" cubes
Vegetable oil for frying

In a heavy gauge pot combine the chili flakes, ketchup, paprika, sugar, water, and vinegar. Cook on a low heat for 30 minutes or until the mixture has reduced by half. Stir in the slurry and bring to a simmer until the sauce has thickened and set aside.

To create the batter, in a separate bowl combine the cornstarch, flour, baking powder, and salt. Whisk in the water until combined, with no lumps. Let the batter rest for three minutes. Pat the fish cubes dry, dredge them in the reserved flour, and place them in the batter until fully coated. In a small saucepot, add half-an-inch of vegetable oil and heat to 375 degrees. Fry the fish until golden brown for about 2-3 minutes. Place on a paper towel to remove any excess oil. Place chili sauce in a bowl and glaze the fish. To serve add additional sauce on the side for dipping.

Chef's Tip: Make sure to only fry a few pieces at a time because batter has a tendency to stick together.

Smoked Salmon Corn Fritters with Roasted-Jalapeno-Pepper Aioli

Serves: 6

½ cup smoked salmon, blood line removed, diced
    (about 4 oz.)
2 tbsp. red peppers, small dice
½ cup sautéed corn off the cob
1 cup + 2 tbsp. flour
1 tsp. baking powder
2 tsp. salt
1 tsp. garlic powder
¼ cup cayenne pepper
¾ cup coffee rich or non-dairy creamer
Vegetable oil for frying
See page 199 for Roasted-Jalapeno-Pepper Aioli recipe

In a bowl combine all the ingredients except for the coffee rich. Once combined, slowly add the coffee rich, making sure there are no lumps. In a small saucepot, add half-an-inch of vegetable oil and heat to 375 degrees. Quenelle one-and-a–half-tablespoon portions of the mixture and fry for 2 minutes or until golden brown. Serve with roasted-jalapeno-pepper aioli.

Southern Fried Popcorn Chicken

Serves: 6

1 lb. skinless and boneless chicken thighs

1 egg

3 tbsp. Frank's RedHot Sauce

2 cups all purpose flour

1½ tbsp. garlic powder

3 tbsp. butcher ground pepper

2 tsp. kosher salt

1 quart vegetable oil for frying

Rinse the chicken and pat dry. Cut the chicken into bite-size pieces, about half an inch thick. In a mixing bowl combine the egg, hot sauce, and chicken, and let the chicken marinate for 30 minutes on the side or for two hours in the refrigerator. Combine the flour, garlic powder, ground pepper, and salt. Remove the chicken from the marinade, shake off any extra egg mixture, and dredge in the flour mixture. In a large skillet preheat oil to 375 degrees. Use a deep fry thermometer for this. Hot oil can be very dangerous, so pay attention to your fry thermometer. Gently fry the chicken in the oil until golden brown and crispy.

Chef's Tip: *Serve with Chef David's Signature BBQ Sauce (see page 188) or the Horseradish Dressing (see page 184). It's great for Super Bowl Sunday!*

Chicken and Waffle Nuggets with Maple Syrup Dip

Serves: 5-6
Yields: 40 nuggets

1 tsp. salt
2 cups flour
3 tbsp. sugar
3½ tsp. baking powder
½ tsp. cinnamon
1 egg yolk
1¼ cup + 2 tbsp. soy milk or non-dairy creamer
½ cup extra-light olive oil
½ tsp. vanilla
1 lb. chicken breast, cut into 1" cubes
3 tbsp. flour (for dredging)
Vegetable oil for frying
Maple syrup dip
Finely chopped chives for garnish

In a mixing bowl combine salt, 2 cups of flour, sugar, baking powder, and cinnamon. In a separate bowl, mix the egg yolk, soy milk or non dairy creamer, extra-light olive oil, and vanilla. Add the wet ingredients to the dry ingredients and stir until there are no lumps.

In a separate mixing bowl, dredge the chicken nuggets in the dredging flour, shake off excess flour, and dip into the waffle mixture. In a small saucepot, add half-an-inch of vegetable oil and heat to 375 degrees. Fry the chicken nuggets for 3-5 minutes or until golden brown. Remove from the oil and let cool on a paper towel to remove excess oil. Serve with your favorite maple syrup for dipping. You can either toss in a bowl with maple syrup or serve on the side and garnish with finely chopped chives.

Short Rib Empanadas with Mango Coulis Dipping Sauce

In 2003 we began preparations to open the Prime Grill in Miami. I flew down to Miami to see the space and begin my recipe development. I wanted to merge the Prime Grill steakhouse concept with the local flavors found in Miami. I decided the best way to do this was to combine one of my best-selling dishes with a classic Latin-inspired item, and so came my short rib empanadas. I added a cooling dip to finish the empanadas, which worked well in sunny Miami, and the dish did so well that we added it to our Prime Grill menu in New York City.

Serves: 6

Yields: 12-15 empanadas

Short Ribs

¾ lb. boneless, uncooked, short rib meat

Salt and pepper to taste

1 pint red wine (Cabernet recommended)

1 pint chicken stock

1 bay leaf

2 sprigs thyme

1 mild jalapeno (seedless and ribless)

2 tbsp. vegetable oil

See page 189 for Mango Coulis recipe.

Puff Pastry

1 package frozen puff pastry dough, thawed (you will
   need 1-2 sheets)

3 tbsp. vegetable oil

1 onion, small dice

3 garlic cloves, minced

1 cup red pepper, small dice

1 cup yellow pepper, small dice

¼ tsp. salt

¼ tsp. powdered chicken base

1 egg (for egg wash)

Short Ribs

Preheat the oven to 325 degrees. Pat the meat dry and season with salt and pepper on both sides. Sear the meat in a heavy gauge pot (braising pot) on each side for one minute until brown, add the rest of the ingredients to the pot, and cover. Place the pot in the oven for three hours (check every 45 minutes to turn the meat so that it cooks evenly) and cook until fork tender. Remove the meat and allow to cool. Reserve the cooking liquid, but remove the jalapeno, thyme, and bay leaf. Shred the meat with the back of a fork and reserve.

Puff Pastry

Preheat the oven to 350 degrees. In a saucepot combine oil, onion, and garlic, and sweat until soft and translucent. Add the red and yellow peppers, salt, and chicken base and cook for 3 minutes. Add the shredded short ribs and a ½ cup of the reserved braising liquid. Bring to a simmer and cook until the mixture is fairly dry. Allow to cool. Roll out puff pastry on a floured surface. Cut out circles with a 3-inch diameter. Place short rib mixture in the center of each puff pastry circle; use approximately 1-2 teaspoons for each. Brush half the edge of each circle with the egg wash, then fold the dough over the meat and seal the edges. Brush the outside of the empanada with egg wash and bake for 20 minutes. Serve with mango coulis for dipping.

Appetizers

When Joey opened the Prime Grill his vision was not to create a traditional Jewish menu filled with brisket and potatoes, gefilte fish, and borscht. He wanted a sophisticated menu that focused on high quality ingredients. Aside from the daily menu, Chef David and Joey create special menu items for a number of Jewish holidays including Rosh Hashanah, Passover, and Chanukah. Passover is always a very hectic, but gratifying, time for the Prime Grill. The kitchen takes weeks to prepare and clean and we change over our entire dining room and menu for a full Kosher for Passover experience.

The first year that we opened, and every year since, we have hosted a Passover Seder at the Prime Grill. I remember at the first Seder we did more than 200 covers the first night and another 180 the second, and I was blown away. The feedback that we received after the meal was that the customers loved the food, but they asked for gefilte fish. I thought to myself, I cooked a delicious meal and all the customer had to say was that they wanted a bottom feeder dish instead? The next day I asked Chaim to pick up a good piece of gefilte fish for me to try from his local kosher food store. I have to admit, there is something quite tasty about gefilte fish, but I knew that I couldn't serve it to my customers in that manner. So I came up with a way to deliver the same flavor and texture of the gefilte fish, but in a more sophisticated manner. The Seafood Quenelle wrapped in Smoked Salmon was served the following year at the Passover Seder and I have since never been asked to replace it with a traditional gefilte fish.

Pineapple Vegetable Strudel

Serves: 8-10

4 tbsp. extra-light olive oil

¼ cup shallots, minced

1 tbsp. garlic, minced

1½ tbsp. curry powder

½ tsp. paprika

¼ tsp. cayenne pepper

½ cup yellow squash, brunoise

½ cup zucchini, brunoise

¼ cup yellow peppers, brunoise

¼ cup red peppers, brunoise

¼ cup pineapple, small dice

½ tsp. salt

1 tsp. flour

¼ cup water

1 heaping tbsp. pareve cream cheese

1 tbsp. cilantro, chopped

1 package frozen puff pastry, thawed

Egg wash

2 sprigs fresh thyme

In a medium-size sauté pan, heat oil and sweat the shallots and garlic until soft and translucent. Add the curry powder, paprika, and cayenne pepper, allowing the spices to bloom and become aromatic. Add the squash, zucchini, yellow pepper, red pepper, and pineapple and season with salt. Sautee the mixture and dust with flour. Add water and cook the mixture down to bind together. Remove from the heat and mix in the cream cheese and cilantro. Allow the mixture to cool. Lightly flour a baking sheet and cut the puff pastry lengthwise into three, two-inch-wide strips and three, two-and-a-half-inch-wide strips. Apply egg wash to the two-inch strips. Place the cooled filling all along the center of the two-inch, egg-washed strips and make sure to leave the edges clear. Place the two and a half-inch strip over the filling and gently crimp the edges using your hands or a fork. Refrigerate the strips for 30 minutes. Meanwhile, preheat the oven to 350 degrees. Remove pastry from the refrigerator and brush the top with egg wash. For additional seasoning, sprinkle some fresh thyme. Score the top with a knife and place in the oven for 10 to 12 minutes or until golden brown and crispy. Cut into one-inch pieces and serve.

Prime Grill Risotto with Truffle Oil and Mushroom Ragout

Serves: 4-6

Mushroom Ragout

2 tbsp. vegetable oil

½ lb. shiitake mushrooms, quartered, stems removed

½ lb. cremini mushrooms, quartered

½ cup shallots, finely minced

3 oz. brandy

2 cups chicken stock

Salt to taste

Risotto

2 tbsp. vegetable oil

½ cup onions, small dice

1 cup Arborio rice

½ cup dry white wine

3 cups chicken stock, hot

1 tbsp. kosher salt

1 tbsp. white truffle oil

Roasted tomato for garnish (optional)

Mushroom Ragout

Heat oil in a sauté pan over medium-heat and gently cook the mushrooms until they start to sweat. Add the shallots to the mushrooms and continue cooking until the natural liquid from the mushrooms has reduced to nothing. Remove mushrooms and shallots from the heat and add brandy. Be sure to do this off the fire to prevent flambé. Place the pan back on the heat and reduce by half. After brandy has reduced, add the chicken stock and reduce by three-fourths. Season the mushroom ragout with salt. Remove from heat and reserve half of the cooked mushrooms. With the other half of the mushrooms and the liquid, blend in the food processor until smooth. Set aside the reserved mushrooms and puree for later.

Risotto

In a heavy gauge stainless steel saucepot, heat the vegetable oil and sweat the onions until soft and translucent. Add the Arborio rice and gently toast for 3-4 minutes, coating each granule in the oil. Season with a pinch of salt. Add the white wine and with a wooden spoon continually stir until the rice absorbs the wine. Slowly start to add the warm chicken stock to the rice half a cup at a time, until the rice is cooked and no stock remains. Make sure to continuously stir the rice to ensure it cooks evenly, doesn't scorch, and most importantly gets creamy. Add the set-aside puree mixture to the rice and bring it back up to temperature. Gently fold in the white truffle oil. Adjust seasonings if necessary. Serve risotto on individual plates or family style and top with reserved mushrooms. Garnish with roasted tomato if desired.

"Crab" Cakes with Horseradish Aioli

One of the most exciting parts of my job is creating dishes that I know my customers can't get anywhere else. The process of developing a brand new dish or, more specifically, a dish that doesn't have typical kosher ingredients, can be quite challenging. It is the challenges in my job that make me a better chef.

One of the staple dishes at the 21 Club was a Maryland-style crab cake. I spent weeks trying to figure out a way to get the texture and flavor of a true crab cake, and with the help of my Mashgiach we were able to find the surimi imitation crabmeat. Through various substitutions and a trial and error period, the dish finally came together. After putting it on the menu, one of my very good customers, Martin Hyman, came into the restaurant with a friend who did not keep kosher. I served them my latest dish and Martin's friend was particularly blown away, which I took as a huge compliment. This is a dish I am very proud of.

Serves: 4
Yields: 4, 3-oz. cakes

"Crab" Cakes

4 oz. imitation crabmeat, chopped fine (surimi brand)
7 oz. cooked cod, no bones or skin
⅛ tsp. cayenne pepper
1 tbsp. cilantro, chopped
1 small garlic clove, minced
1 tbsp. jalapeno pepper, no seeds or rib, fine dice
2 oz. mayonnaise
1½ tsp. Old Bay seasoning
1½ tsp. red peppers, no seeds or rib, fine dice
1½ tsp. yellow peppers, no seeds or rib, fine dice
2 cups bread crumbs
2 tbsp. vegetable oil for frying
See page 185 for Horseradish Aioli recipe

In a mixing bowl, combine the imitation crab and cooked cod fish and lightly mix. The cod should be flaked. Add the remaining ingredients to the mixing bowl (except the bread crumbs) and with a rubber spatula gently mix until fully incorporated. Divide the mixture into four even parts and with your hands form four, three-ounce cakes or patties. Coat and pack each patty tightly with breadcrumbs. Let the crab cakes set in the refrigerator for two to three hours. Preheat the oven to 350 degrees. In a medium size non-stick skillet over medium-high heat, add two tablespoons of oil and cook the cakes on all sides until golden brown. Place the cakes in a glass baking dish and finish in the oven for 8 minutes. Serve the crab cakes over a two-ounce dollop of horseradish dressing and garnish with sliced avocado or guacamole.

THE PRIME GRILL COOKBOOK

Seafood Quenelle with Five-Herb Aioli

Serves: 4
Yields: 12 Sausages

2 lbs. sea bass, small dice
8 egg whites
¼ cup tarragon, finely chopped (stems removed)
¼ cup Italian parsley, finely chopped (stems removed)
1 tsp. nutmeg
½ tsp. cardamom
1 tsp. Old Bay seasoning
½ tsp. white pepper
2 tsp. salt
½ quart Five-Herb Aioli (*See page 197 for recipe*)

Preheat the oven to 350 degrees. In a food processor with the blade attachment, process the sea bass until smooth and add the remaining ingredients. Process until the mixture is fully combined. On a baking sheet lined with parchment paper, scoop 12 quenelles of the mixture and bake for 12 minutes. Serve with Five-Herb Aioli.

Chef's Tip: For Passover, wrap the quenelle in smoked salmon and serve with horseradish dressing.

Mediterranean Tuna Tartar

Serves: 6-8

1 lb. sashimi-quality tuna, small dice
1 cup green apples, small dice
½ cup cucumbers, small dice
½ cup scallions
1 tsp. salt
4 tbsp. Mediterranean Dressing *(See page 182 for recipe)*
Fresh cracked black pepper to taste

Combine all ingredients in a bowl with 4 tablespoons of dressing and serve over a crostini or rosemary potato chips. Garnish with toasted almonds (if desired).

Chef's Tip: *Dressing goes very well with arugula.*

Salmon Tartar

Serves: 4

1 lb. fresh salmon, small dice
4 tsp. fresh lemon juice
4 tsp. Horseradish Dressing *(See page 184 for recipe)*
2 tbsp. capers (no liquid)
4 tsp. olive oil
1 tsp. lemon zest
4 tbsp. scallions, finely chopped
1 tsp. salt
Pepper to taste

Combine all ingredients in a mixing bowl. Adjust seasoning if needed. Serve with Belgian endive spears or a toasted baguette.

Chef's Tip: *Do not let the mixture sit for a long time, or the marinade will cook the fish.*

Seafood Ceviche

Serves: 4

1 lb. fresh, lean white fish or salmon, small dice
⅓ cup lime juice
⅓ cup extra virgin olive oil
3 tbsp. jalapeno pepper, minced (approximately
    2 peppers)
1 cup seeded plum tomatoes, small diced
⅓ cup shallots, minced
⅓ cup scallions, finely chopped
⅔ cup tomato juice
¼ cup cilantro, finely chopped
½ tsp. salt
¼ tsp. hot sauce (Tabasco preferred)
½ cup cucumbers deseeded, small dice

In a mixing bowl, mix all of the ingredients and let marinate for three minutes. Serve in a martini glass over guacamole for a contrast in flavor.

Chef's Tip: *Take a small piece of the jalapeno and taste to measure the level of heat.*

Mojito-Cured Salmon with Mojo Sauce and Marinated Tomatoes

This dish was a dish that I conceptualized while I was down in Miami. I wanted to create my own version of smoked salmon without the smoke, better known as gravlax. What is so great about this dish is that it is easy to make at home and it can be enjoyed in a multitude of ways.

Serves: 4-6

Special Equipment:
Cheesecloth
Butcher's twine

Mojito-Cured Salmon
2, 8-10 oz. pieces fresh salmon fillet, skin on
2 tbsp. whole coriander
1 tbsp. whole black peppercorns
1 lemon, juiced & zested (separate the juice and zest)
1 lime, juiced & zested (separate the juice and zest)
1 orange, juiced & zested (separate the juice and zest)
2 cups brown sugar
3 tbsp. cilantro, coarsely chopped
1 cup salt
¼ cup dark tequila

Mojo Sauce
1 cup extra virgin olive oil
1 tbsp. garlic, chopped
1 tsp. salt
1 tbsp. lime juice
3 tbsp. white vinegar
2 tbsp. parsley, chopped
2 tbsp. cilantro, chopped

Mojito-Cured Salmon

Place the two pieces of salmon skin-side-down on a cheesecloth. In a small mixing bowl combine the coriander, black peppercorns, citrus zest, brown sugar, cilantro, and salt and disperse evenly on both pieces of salmon. Combine the lemon, lime, orange juice, and tequila and drizzle the mixture over the dry ingredients. Carefully sandwich the two pieces of salmon together, flesh on flesh. The skin side should be facing outward. Twist the sides of the cheesecloth in opposite directions (similar to a candy wrapper) to tightly wrap the salmon and secure at each end with butcher's twine. Place the salmon on a sheet tray in the refrigerator and cover with a heavy plate. Leave the salmon in the refrigerator for 36 hours, turning the salmon over every 12 hours. Remove the cheesecloth and rinse the fish off in cold water. Pat dry and slice paper thin.

Mojo Sauce

In a small pot place olive oil, garlic, and salt over medium heat. Once the aroma starts to build, add the lime juice and vinegar and bring to a simmer. Don't brown the garlic. Remove from the heat and let cool. Once cool, add the parsley and cilantro.

Marinated Tomatoes

Combine all ingredients and let marinate for two to three minutes.

Marinated Tomatoes

1 ripe beefsteak tomato, skin on, seeds removed, small dice

1 medium shallot, minced

1 tbsp. extra virgin olive oil

2 tsp. balsamic vinegar

¼ tsp. salt

¼ tsp. pepper

Assembly

To serve, slice the cured salmon and garnish with the mojo sauce and marinated tomatoes. This dish is served best with a side of tortilla or plantain chips.

Chef's Tip: It is important to use a sharp carving knife that is long and narrow to evenly and thinly slice the salmon.

Thai Peanut Satay

Serves: 6

Special Equipment:
Wooden skewers

Marinade
1 cup water
1 tbsp. curry powder
½ tsp. cayenne pepper
1 cup smooth peanut butter
½ tsp. salt
1 heaping tbsp. garlic, minced
1 ½ lbs. boneless, skinless chicken breast

Dipping Sauce
1 cup marinade
¼ cup mayonnaise
2 tsp. white vinegar
¼ cup scallions, garnish (optional)

In a saucepot over medium heat, place water, curry powder, and cayenne pepper and reduce to ¾ cup; remove from the stove. In a mixing bowl pour the hot water and spice mixture over the peanut butter, salt, and garlic. Using a whisk, stir the mixture until evenly combined. Set aside one cup of the marinade for the dipping sauce. Slice the chicken length wise into four-inch-long strips. With the remaining marinade, marinate the chicken in a plastic bag in the refrigerator for two hours. While the chicken is marinating, soak the wooden skewers in water to prevent them from burning. Remove the chicken from the marinade and skewer the chicken lengthwise so that they resemble lollipops. The skewers can be baked or grilled. To grill, place over a lightly oiled medium-high-heat grill, and grill on each side for two minutes or until done. To bake, place in the oven on a lightly oiled baking sheet at 350 degrees for 9-10 minutes.

Dipping Sauce

In a mixing bowl, combine the reserved cup of marinade, ¼ cup of mayonnaise, and 2 tsps. of white vinegar; whisk until smooth. To serve, accompany the chicken with the dipping sauce and garnish with chopped scallions.

Steak Tartar

Every steakhouse has to have a steak tartar. Instead of grinding our meat we dice the meat by hand.

Serves: 2-3

8 oz. lean prime filet steak, small dice
1 tbsp. sweet relish
2 tbsp. shallots, minced
2 tbsp. olive oil
2 tbsp. capers, chopped
1 tsp. spicy dijon mustard
1 egg yolk
3 tbsp. loosely packed flat leaf parsley, chopped
¼ tsp. salt

In a mixing bowl, combine all ingredients and mix to ensure fully combined. Serve on garlic toast or with rosemary potato chips.

Chef's Tip: *Always use a lean cut of meat with very little connective tissue and fat.*

THE PRIME GRILL COOKBOOK

Potato Gnocchi with Duck Bolognaise and Sage

Serves: 8
Yields: 2 Quarts Duck Bolognaise

Potato Gnocchi

2½ lbs. Idaho potatoes (approximately 3 large potatoes)
1 small bunch rosemary, stems removed and chopped
4-5 garlic cloves, roughly sliced
2 tbsp. extra virgin olive oil
Salt and white pepper to taste
1 cup all purpose flour
2 egg yolks

Duck Bolognaise

1 cup carrots, small dice
1 cup celery, small dice
1 cup onion, small dice
⅓ cup olive oil
5-7 garlic cloves, thinly sliced
1½ lbs. ground duck meat
3 tbsp. tomato paste
1 bay leaf
2 tsp. dry thyme
2 tsp. dry sage
1 tbsp. dry basil
1 tbsp. garlic powder
1 cup white wine (Pinot Grigio)
1 cup chicken stock
1 cup veal stock
1 quart canned, peeled plum tomatoes, roughly cut
Salt and pepper to taste

Potato Gnocchi

Preheat the oven to 350 degrees. Clean the potatoes with the skin on and dry well. In a bowl, combine the potatoes with the rosemary, garlic, and extra virgin olive oil. Season with salt and pepper and coat the potatoes well. Place on a baking tray and bake in the oven for approximately one hour, or until fork tender. Remove from the oven and let cool. Peel the potatoes and pulse them in a food processor with the grater attachment. Set aside the potatoes to continue to cool. When potatoes are room temperature, combine with the flour, egg yolks, and salt and pepper to taste. Knead the potatoes with your hands until combined, being careful not to overwork the dough. On a clean, lightly floured surface, roll out the dough into logs, with a half-inch diameter, and cut the logs into three-fourth-inch pieces. After gnocchi is cut, cook the gnocchi in boiling salted water. When the gnocchi float to the top, they are done.

Duck Bolognaise

In a heavy gauge saucepot, preferably stainless steel, cook the carrots, celery, and onions in the olive oil over medium heat until soft and translucent. Add the sliced garlic and cook the garlic until aromatic. Turn up the heat to high, add the ground duck meat, and brown. Add all of the dried herbs and deglaze with the white wine. Reduce by half. Add both stocks and the tomatoes and simmer slowly for 45 minutes, skimming the grease with a ladle as often as possible. Season with salt and pepper and remove the bay leaf. Serve the bolognaise with a heaping portion of gnocchi.

Chef's Tip: Potatoes must be cooled when the flour is added to the potatoes to get a light and airy gnocchi. Do not overwork the potatoes in the food processor or when mixing by hand with the eggs and flour in order to achieve an aerated gnocchi. You can brown the gnocchi with olive oil infused with rosemary or garlic by sautéing them for a minute or two with the flavored extra virgin olive oil.

Chef's Tip: *The quantity of flour needed can differ depending on the moisture content of the potato and the humidity found in your kitchen or the time of the year. Adjust as necessary.*

Chef's Tip: *The skins of the potatoes are great if deep-fried, salted, and served as a side! I do this at the Prime Grill.*

Lamb Turnovers

The majority of my dishes are conceptualized from inspirations around me—generally seasonal ingredients, methods I learned from school and mentors, and flavor profiles I want to emulate and make better. But, occasionally I get inspired by fully creating a dish from nothing. One afternoon at the Prime Grill, I had leftover lamb meat and wanted to be able to use the meat in some way. The obvious choice would have been to incorporate the meat into a burger, but I pushed myself and with the idea of a dish I had during past travels, I created a new dish—a flavorful lamb turnover.

Serves: 12-14
Yields: 28 turnovers

2 tbsp. extra virgin olive oil
2 tbsp. extra light olive oil
1 cup onions, small dice
1 tbsp. garlic, minced
2 tbsp. curry powder
⅛ tsp. cardamom
¼ tsp. nutmeg
¼ tsp. cumin
¾ tsp. cinnamon
½ tsp. paprika
½ tsp. salt
⅛ tsp. black pepper
1 lb. lean ground lamb
1 box filo dough, thawed
1 stick margarine, melted

Preheat the oven to 350 degrees. In a medium-sauté pan, heat oil and sweat the onions until soft and translucent. Add the garlic, curry powder, cardamom, nutmeg, cumin, cinnamon, paprika, salt, and pepper and allow the spices to bloom on medium-low heat. Once bloomed add the lamb. Stir and break up the lamb meat until the meat is browned. To create the turnover you need to allow the meat to cool. As the meat is cooling, thaw the filo dough and melt the margarine. Place three layers of filo dough together and brush each layer with a nice coating of margarine to adhere each layer. Cut the layered dough into three-inch strips and place the strips so that they are vertical. Brush the edges of the strips with margarine. Place one tablespoon of lamb in the bottom left corner of the strip and fold the dough over to form a triangle, as you would to fold a flag. Continue folding until you seal the triangle completely. Remove excess dough and brush the top with margarine. Bake in the oven for 10-12 minutes or until golden brown.

Chef's Tip: The filling is already fully cooked before we put it in the dough so be careful not to over cook. We are just browning the pastry. When working with filo dough, the dough tends to dry out quickly. To avoid, place a damp towel over the dough that you are not using.

Lamb Meatballs with White Bean, Curry, and Basil Sauce

With the help of our public relations and marketing director, we have had many opportunities to appear in the press, especially to lend our expertise during the Jewish holiday season. I created this dish specifically for a Tony Tantillo segment on CBS.

Serves: 6

1 small onion, minced
¼ cup extra-light olive oil
2 cloves garlic
½ tsp. paprika
⅛ tsp. tumeric
⅛ tsp. cumin
⅛ tsp. cayenne pepper
¼ tsp. cinnamon
⅛ tsp. ground clove
½ tsp. ground cardamom
¼ tsp. salt
⅛ tsp. ginger powder
1 pinch saffron (optional)
1½ lb lean ground lamb meat
1 egg
½ cup breadcrumbs
See page 190 for White Bean, Curry, and Basil Sauce recipe

In a sauté pan, cook the onions in extra-light olive oil until soft and translucent. Add the garlic and when you begin to smell the garlic, add the remaining spices. Cook for three minutes on low heat or until the spice mixture is bloomed and the aromas open up. Remove from the heat and allow to cool. In a bowl combine the lamb, egg, spices, and breadcrumbs and mix until combined. Roll into one-inch meatballs and cook with oil in a sauté pan until golden brown or bake in a 350 degree oven for 10 to 15 minutes. To serve, place three to four lamb meatballs on a plate and add the White Bean, Curry, and Basil Sauce. Garnish with chopped mint, basil, and pepper flakes.

Soups

Everyone has a favorite dish from his or her grandmother and I am no different. When I first came to the Prime Grill, Joey wanted me to help elevate the menu, but he also wanted to create a menu that was relatable and featured home-style flavors that people cherished. The best way I knew to achieve this was to add a chicken soup. I took my grandmother's basic recipe and enhanced it with a little sherry wine and implemented a long cooking process to concentrate the flavors. I often get remarks from customers that the chicken soup is one of their favorite dishes on the menu.

English Pea and Mint Soup

Serves: 6

Special Equipment:
Cheesecloth or coffee filter
Butcher's twine

½ cup leeks, small dice
½ cup celery, small dice
1 cup onions, small dice
1½ quarts chicken stock (vegetable stock can be substituted)
1 sachet bag (3 sprigs of thyme, 1 crushed bay leaf, 1 tsp. crushed peppercorns)
1½ quarts fresh peas (frozen can be used if fresh are not available)
5 tbsp. mint, chiffonade
Salt and pepper to taste
Dollop of pareve sour cream, optional

In a heavy gauged saucepot over medium heat, sweat the leeks, celery, and onion until soft and translucent. Add the chicken stock and sachet bag and bring mixture to a simmer for 8-10 minutes. Remove the sachet bag and add the fresh peas. Continue cooking for 5 minutes until the peas are soft, but remain vibrant in color. Add the mint, remove from the heat, place over an ice bath, and let the soup cool (stir to expedite the cooling process.) In a blender, blend the soup until smooth. Add salt and pepper to taste. Serve chilled and garnish with fresh mint, extra virgin olive oil, and a dollop of pareve sour cream.

Chef's Tip: This soup can be served chilled or warm.

Corn Chowder

The three things that make a chowder are potatoes, cream, and some type of swine. Two of the three items I was not able to use, because dairy cream can't be served at a kosher meat restaurant and swine animals are not kosher altogether. I had to therefore be resourceful and adapt flavors that would mimic the flavors I couldn't use. I created this dish as a transitional soup great for serving near the end of winter and into spring.

Yields: 2 Quarts

4 oz. margarine, cut in 2 2-oz. pieces
1 cup beef fry, small dice
1 cup Spanish onions, small dice
2 cups corn, off the cob (reserve cobs if using fresh corn)
½ cup celery, small dice
1 cup seedless and ribless red peppers, small dice
1 cup seedless and ribless yellow peppers, small dice
2 cups Idaho potatoes, small dice
½ cup all purpose flour
1½ quart chicken stock
1 cup non dairy creamer or soy milk (rich's creamer)
1 tbsp. kosher salt
1 pinch cayenne pepper to taste
Chives, chopped (garnish)
Chili oil (garnish)

If using fresh corn, add the cobs to the chicken stock and steep over low heat to infuse the flavor.

In a heavy gauged pot, preferably stainless steel, add half of the margarine and melt over medium heat. Add the beef fry and cook to render out the fat and until crispy. Add the onions and corn and cook until the onions become soft and translucent, and the corn takes on a bright yellow hue. Add the celery and red and yellow peppers and cook for another two minutes. Add the potatoes and the second half of the margarine and cook for an additional two minutes. Add the flour and stir well with a wooden spoon, being careful not to brown the flour. Slowly stir in the chicken stock. If using a fortified corn stock, pull the cobs out. (Add the stock in three or four parts. After each part is added, bring to a simmer to let the mixture thicken while making sure there are no lumps.) Simmer for one hour. Temper in the creamer and add the salt and cayenne pepper. Bring to a simmer and serve. To serve, garnish the soup with chopped chives and chili oil.

Chef's Tip: If using soy milk, be careful because the milk will curdle if it gets too hot.

Grandma Bella's Chicken Soup

Serves: 6

Special Equipment:
Cheesecloth
Butcher's twine

2 cups white onions, diced
1 cup leeks (use only the white part), diced
1 cup carrots, diced
1 cup celery
1½ cups sherry wine
6 cups chicken stock
1, 3½ lb. whole broiler chicken cut into 8 pieces,
    rinsed and cleaned
Sachet bag (3 sprigs thyme, 1 bay leaf, 1 tsp. crushed
    peppercorns, 3 sprigs Italian parsley stems, 1 small
    bunch fresh dill, 2 garlic cloves smashed)
Salt and pepper to taste
Dill, chopped (garnish)
Peas (optional)
Green and yellow zucchini (optional)

In a soup pot, sweat the onions, leeks, carrots, and celery until soft and translucent. Add the sherry wine and bring to a simmer to release some of the alcohol. Add the chicken stock, chicken and sachet bag, bring to a boil, and immediately lower to a lazy bubble for two hours. Constantly skim the foam and grease. Remove the chicken, put aside, and let cool. After the chicken cools, with your fingers remove the skin and bones and shred the chicken. (For a warm, rustic, family feel, leave the chicken on the bone.) Add the shredded chicken to the broth and add salt and pepper to taste. Garnish with fresh chopped dill and serve with lots of love. You can also use peas and green and yellow zucchini or other vegetables of your choice for additional color and nutrients.

Porcini Mushroom Soup

Serves: 4-6

½ cup extra-light olive oil
2 cups onion, small dice
½ cup celery, small dice
2 garlic cloves, minced
2½ cups defrosted frozen porcini mushrooms, rough
   chopped (reserve defrosted liquid)
½ cup all purpose flour
6 cups liquid (defrosted liquid + chicken stock to equal
   6 cups)
1 tbsp. salt
1 cup pareve cream cheese
Caramelized onions (optional)

In a heavy guage soup pot, heat extra-light olive oil and sweat the onions and celery until soft and translucent. Add the garlic and cook until aromatic. Add the porcini mushrooms and stir in the flour and cook for another three to four minutes. Add the liquid slowly, working out any lumps from the flour and add salt. Once the liquid is combined bring to a boil and immediately lower to a simmer on low heat for a half hour, stirring constantly to prevent burning. Add the pareve cream cheese and combine till smooth. Remove from the heat and let the mixture cool. Puree in a blender until smooth. Serve with croutons or a toasted piece of bread and garnish with caramelized onions.

Chef's Tip: Because you are working with a roux, you want to add the water slowly. So that there are no lumps, use a whisk to ensure proper incorporation. In addition, because it is a thick soup, it should be stirred very frequently.

THE PRIME GRILL COOKBOOK

Spicy Sausage and Chicken Gumbo

I was at home cooking during Hurricane Irene two years ago and my wife Jennifer and I decided to have a hurricane party and keep ourselves busy. Jennifer is from the south and to show our southern hospitality we created this dish together.

Serves: 8

1, 3-lb. chicken cut into 8 pieces, skin off

Salt and pepper to taste

1½-2 lbs. Jack's Gourmet chorizo sausage, cut into
    ¼-inch round slices

1 cup vegetable oil

1 cup all purpose flour

3 small Spanish onions, small dice

2 large red bell peppers, small dice, seedless and ribs
    removed

3 stalks celery, small dice

5 cloves garlic, minced

4 quarts cold chicken stock (or water)

1 bay leaf

5 tsp. Cajun or Creole seasonings (recommend Paul
    Prudhomme's Magic)

1½ tsp. dried thyme

1 tbsp. + 2 tsp. gumbo filé powder

3 cups okra, ¼-inch slices

½ tsp. cayenne pepper

1 cup finely chopped scallions

½ cup chopped flat leaf parsley

Rinse the chicken and pat dry. Season the chicken with salt and pepper. In a sauté pan, brown the chicken on all sides and remove. Add the sausage and brown on all sides and set aside with the chicken. Deglaze the pan with half a cup of water or cold stock and reserve the mixture. In a heavy gauge soup pot over medium-to-high heat add oil and flour. (This is the beginning of a dark Cajun roux.) Constantly stir until the roux begins to turn the color of coffee, which could take 45 minutes to one hour. Please note how important this step is as it is the base of the entire dish and the foundation of all flavor. Add the vegetables (onion, peppers, celery) to the roux; the vegetables will cook very quickly due to the hot temperature of the roux. After the vegetables have cooked for about three to five minutes, slowly whisk in the cold chicken stock with the deglazed water (previously set aside) in four parts to avoid lumps. Add all ingredients other than scallions and parsley and simmer for one hour, constantly degreasing with a ladle. Stir in the scallions and parsley before serving. This dish can be served over rice.

Chef's Tip: Put the pot half off the burner so that the grease is forced to one side of the pot and be careful not to burn yourself, as the roux will get extremely hot.

Salads

Healthy eating is an important aspect of the Prime Grill. Joey generally comes into the restaurant towards the end of lunch or dinner service famished and on most days heads to the meat station. But in the past couple of years, I often found Joey asking for arugula and olives. Therefore, Joey inspired me to create the Mediterranean Salad, which satisfied not only a healthy dish, but also flavors that are reminiscent of his roots.

Chef's Tip: Before mixing your salad contents put dressing on the side of the bowl. When you introduce your greens, lightly mix the salad to avoiding bruising the delicate greens.

The Prime Grill Salad

Serves: 4

8 cups romaine lettuce, cut into 1" strips, width wise

2 cups sliced, seedless cucumbers, cut into half
   moons

2 cups croutons

1 cup yellow tomatoes, large dice

1 cup red tomatoes, large dice

1 cup red onions, small dice

¾ cup Lemon Vinaigrette Dressing *(See page 180 for
   recipe)*

In a large mixing bowl, combine all ingredients and serve individually or family style. Dress the salad with the lemon vinaigrette dressing.

Mediterranean Salad

Serves: 4-6

6 cups arugula, loosely packed
¾ cup red onion, finely sliced
1 cup pepperoni, thinly sliced (or any dry sausage)
1 cup cherry tomatoes, halved
¾ cup sun dried tomatoes, julienned
¼ cup capers
½ cup black olives (Nicoise or Kalamata)
Mediterranean Dressing *(See page 182 for recipe)*

Combine ingredients and lightly dress the salad with desired amount of dressing.

Chef's Tip: *Serve the salad with lamb cigars on top as a garnish.*

Arugula Fennel Salad and Balsamic Reduction

Serves: 4

Salad

4 cups arugula, loosely packed

2 cups fennel, core removed and thinly sliced

½ cup quartered olives (Kalamata or Nicoise)

2 cups cherry tomatoes, halved

¼ cup Lemon Vinaigrette Dressing *(see page 180 for recipe)* fresh lemon juice and extra virgin olive oil can be substituted

Balsamic Reduction

1 cup balsamic vinegar

⅓ cup sugar

Salad

In a large mixing bowl, combine the arugula, fennel, olives, and cherry tomatoes. Add the Lemon Vinaigrette (or olive oil and lemon juice if preferred) and mix well.

Balsamic Reduction

In a saucepot, place the balsamic vinegar and the sugar and bring to a simmer over medium heat. Reduce the liquid by half (approximately 10 minutes) and remove from heat (don't over-reduce; the sauce will thicken after cooling down). If it cooks too much or too quickly, it will burn because of the high sugar content. Serve the salad alone or under our Chicken Milanese and drizzle with the balsamic reduction.

Cobb Salad

Serves: 4-6

1 cup sautéed corn off the cob (fresh or frozen)
6 cups romaine lettuce, shredded
2 cups deseeded plum tomatoes, small dice
½ cup red onion, small dice
1 small avocado, small dice
2½ cups turkey pastrami, small dice or grilled chicken
Horseradish Dressing *(see page 184 for recipe)*

Mix lettuce, tomatoes, corn, onion, avocado, and turkey or chicken in a bowl, and dress salad to your liking.

Boston Salad with Jalapeno Ranch Dressing

Serves: 4-6

4 tbsp. beef fry, chopped

2 small heads Boston lettuce, leaves separated and
     torn in half

1 whole avocado, medium dice

1 cup cherry or pear tomatoes, halved

4 tbsp. toasted sunflower seeds

½ sweet white onion, thinly sliced

½ cup Ranch Dressing *(see page 183 for recipe)*

Preheat oven to 325 degrees. Place the beef fry on a sheet pan, and bake for 15 minutes until crispy (flip sides after 8 minutes). Remove from oven and let cool. In a large mixing bowl, mix all of the ingredients including the Ranch Dressing and serve individually or in a large salad bowl. Garnish with an avocado fan and additional crispy beef fry.

Chimichurri Salad

Serves: 4-6

1 lb. boneless, skinless chicken cutlets, small dice after cooking

¼ cup + ¾ cup Chimichurri Dressing/Marinade *(see page 186 for recipe)*

1 avocado, small dice

1 cup cooked black beans

1 cup sautéed or grilled corn off the cob

6 cups mesclun greens, chopped

½ cup red onion, small dice

1 cup deseeded plum tomatoes, small dice

1 soft flour tortilla (optional)

Preheat the oven to 350 degrees. Clean the chicken and pat dry. In a large mixing bowl, place the chicken and ¼ cup of the dressing to fully coat. Cover the chicken and let marinate in a refrigerator for one hour. Remove and bake the chicken in the oven for 9-10 minutes until fully cooked. Dice the chicken and set aside. Combine all of the ingredients including the chicken and dress with ¾ cup of dressing or to your liking. For added crunch, cut a tortilla into two-inch-long julienne strips and deep fry. Let cool and garnish on top of the salad.

ENTREES

Fish

———

Unimpressed by the quality of the fish that was being delivered to the restaurant, Joey wanted to change things and better understand the process of selecting the highest-grade fish. On recommendation, he was told to head to the fish market and see for himself what the fresh catch was each morning. Since that day, Joey has developed a close relationship with many of the fishermen in the market and personally selects, with the assistance of our purchaser, the freshest catches of the day. This is truly a symbol of the dedication he puts into his product selection and the quality he delivers to his customers.

Falafel Crusted Salmon

This dish was created by myself and my friend Aaron Bashy.

Serves: 4

Special Equipment:
Parchment paper

1½ cup cooked chickpeas
¼ cup cilantro, chopped
2 tsp. salt
2 tsp. onion powder
2 tsp. garlic powder
1 tbsp. jalapeno, minced
½ cup panko breadcrumbs
2 tsp. cumin powder
1 egg
4, 7-oz. salmon filets
3 tbsp. extra-light olive oil

Preheat the oven to 350 degrees. In a food processor, place the chickpeas, cilantro, salt, onion powder, garlic powder, jalapeno, panko, cumin, and egg. Combine until the mixture is finely chopped and well mixed. On a clean sheet pan, place a sheet of parchment paper and place the mixture on top. Cover with another piece of parchment paper and role the mixture using a rolling pin, so that the mixture is tightly packed about ¼-inch thick. Gently place the four pieces of the fish fillet on the parchment paper and using a sharp knife, "sketch" the shape of the fillets. Remove the sketch of the crust, peel off the top layer of the parchment paper, and place mixture on top of the corresponding salmon filet. Remove the parchment paper and set the filet aside. Heat three tablespoons of oil in a non stick pan on high heat and sear the salmon fillet with the crust-side down for two minutes, until golden brown. Using a fish spatula, gently flip the fillet and remove from fire. Finish the salmon fillets in the oven for four to five minutes or until desired temperature. Serve this dish with the Arugula and Fennel Salad or the Cobb Salad.

Chef's Tip: When you sear fish or meat, always sear the presentation side first. This will help you achieve a perfect color on the presentation side. When flipping the filet to sear, flip gently so that the crust adheres to the filet.

Teriyaki-Glazed Chilean Sea Bass with Cauliflower Curry Puree

Serves: 4

½ cup soy sauce
½ cup sugar
¼ cup mirin
3 garlic cloves, crushed (use your knife or the bottom of a pot to crush the garlic cloves)
4, 7-oz. fillets sea bass
Salt to taste
2 tbsp. oil
Cauliflower Curry Puree *(see page 145 for recipe)*

Preheat the oven to 350 degrees. In a saucepan over medium heat, combine the soy sauce, sugar, mirin, and crushed garlic cloves. Reduce slowly for approximately 30 minutes until it thickens and coats the back of a spoon; set aside. Season the fish with salt. Add the oil to a heavy gauged frying pan and put on high heat. After the frying pan is hot, sear the fish for 2 minutes on each side. Bake the fish in the oven for 8 to 10 minutes and glaze the top of the fish with the teriyaki after every two minutes. Serve over the Cauliflower Curry Puree.

Tuna Steak Frites, Yucca Fries, Horseradish Zabaglione

Serves: 4

Tuna Steak Frites

2 lb. fresh sashimi quality tuna cut into 4, 8-oz
    portions
4 tbsp. extra-light olive oil
Salt to taste
¾ cup Pepper and Herb Japanese Breadcrumbs
Yucca Fries *(See page 156 for recipe)*
Horseradish Zabaglione *(See page 192 for recipe)*

Pepper and Herb Japanese Breadcrumbs

¾ cup Japanese breadcrumbs (panko)
1 tbsp. butcher ground black pepper
1 tbsp. basil, chiffonade
½ tbsp. chopped fresh oregano

Pepper and Herb Japanese Breadcrumbs

In a bowl, mix all ingredients well and put aside.

Tuna Steak Frites

Lightly brush the tuna with two tablespoons of oil. Season with salt and dredge the tuna in the Pepper and Herb Japanese Breadcrumbs. Place the remaining two tablespoons of oil in a sauté pan and place over a medium heat. When the pan is hot (after two to three minutes), lightly brown the tuna on all sides. Cook until your desired temperature is reached. To serve, place the horseradish zabaglione on the plate in a nice fluid direction and rest the tuna on top, cut in half, and accompany with yucca fries.

Chef's Tip: Medium rare is the preferred temperature. To cook medium and above, the fish should be finished in a 325 degree oven for approximately five to seven minutes.

Red Snapper en Papillote

Serves: 4

Special Equipment:
4 pieces, 12" x 14" parchment paper

2 plum tomatoes, julienned, seeds and insides
   removed
¾ cup basil, chiffonade (approximately 2-3 large
   sprigs)
2 cups fennel, thinly sliced and cored (approximately
   ½ fennel), white portion only
1 yellow pepper, julienned
Juice of 1 lemon
¼ tsp. truffle oil
8 tsp. extra-light olive oil
4, 6-oz. pieces red snapper fillet, skin off (striped bass
   can be substituted)
Salt to taste

Preheat the oven to 350 degrees. In a mixing bowl combine the julienned tomatoes, basil, fennel, yellow pepper, lemon juice, and truffle oil and mix well. Fold each piece of 12 x 14-inch parchment paper in half and cut into a half-heart shape. Open the heart and coat one side with one teaspoon of extra light olive oil. Place the fish on that side and season with salt and the vegetable garnish (¼ portion on each piece of fish.) Fold the other half of the heart over to enclose the fish. Starting at the top of the heart, fold over the edge about a ¼ of an inch around the entire heart to create a tight seal. When the hem reaches the bottom tip of the heart, twist the bottom inch or two to seal tightly. Drizzle one teaspoon of oil over the top of the bag. Place the fish in the oven for 8-10 minutes. The steam will make the parchment paper rise. Place packet on a plate, and with a sharp knife or scissors, carefully cut a large "X" on the top of the packet. Peel back to serve. The fish can be served in the paper or plated, but make sure to use all of the flavorful juices that are left in the parchment!

Chef's Tip: You are creating a vacuum inside of the bag, so to keep the fish moist and to concentrate the flavors it is very important to always seal the bag very tightly.

Pan Seared Red Snapper with Quinoa Pilaf and Lemon Caper Olive Oil

I love this dish not only because of the flavor, but because it truly is good for you. Quinoa is considered a complete protein because it contains all eight essential amino acids and it is considered to be the super grain of the future—I always take great pride in giving my customers not only delicious dishes, but healthy ones too.

Serves: 4

4, 6-oz. fillets red snapper, skin on
2 tbsp. extra light olive oil
Salt and pepper to taste
Quinoa Pilaf *(see page 153 for recipe)*
Lemon Caper Olive Oil *(see page 191 for recipe)*

Rinse the fish and pat dry well. If desired, score the skin with a knife by making two "x" marks; this allows for even cooking and prevents the fish from curling. Heat oil in a non-stick pan on medium-to-high heat. Season the fish with salt and pepper and place in the hot pan, skin-side down. For four to five minutes, baste the top of the fish constantly with a spoon, by holding the pan diagonally toward you, allowing you to scoop the liquid. Position the fish away from you and in the upper half of the pan, so you can baste it easily. Basting allows you to cook a fish skin-side down and keep the top-side moist while delicately cooking. Serve the fish skin-side-up over a bed of Quinoa Pilaf and drizzle the Lemon Caper Olive Oil all over.

Chef's Tip: The key component to this dish is to make sure the skin is crispy. In order to do so you must pat the fish dry and season only moments before cooking while making sure that the pan is very hot.

Meat

Our most famous evening at the Prime Grill is Tuesday's "Delmonico" Night. For weeks Joey was working downstairs in the butcher room, cutting different pieces from the shoulder of the rib eye. Finally, one day he came upstairs with this juicy, thick piece of meat, and asked Chef David to come up with a special sauce for it. That same evening, similar to the evening with the BBQ Duck Spring roles, Chef David made ten orders and sold out immediately. We started serving the steak as a special on a Tuesday evening, which at the time was a slower night for the restaurant. As the dish continued to sell out, an executive decision was made and from henceforth, Tuesdays became Delmonico Night—and subsequently the busiest night of the week.

Whole Roasted Chicken with Rosemary, Mustard, and Soy Crust

Serves: 4

Special Equipment:
Kitchen twine (at least 30 inches)
Pastry brush
Roasting pan

Marinade
¼ cup Dijon mustard
⅛ cup low sodium soy sauce
1 bunch rosemary, removed from the stem, chopped

Mirepoix
1 large white onion, medium dice
2 celery stalks, medium dice
1 carrot, medium dice
1 garlic head, cloves separated, skin on

Roasted Chicken
3½ lb. whole broiler chicken (wingettes removed)
Salt and pepper to taste
1 bunch rosemary
1 bunch thyme
2 bay leaves, hand crushed
1 head garlic, cut in half
1 lemon, cut in half
2-3 tbsp. extra-light olive oil

Gravy
2 tbsp. all purpose flour
2 cups cold chicken stock
1 bunch rosemary
Salt and pepper to taste

Preheat the oven to 450 degrees. In a mixing bowl, combine all the marinade ingredients and mix well. Place all mirepoix ingredients in a roasting pan. Place the chicken on a clean surface and season the cavity with salt and pepper. Stuff the chicken with the rosemary, thyme, bay leaf, garlic head, and lemon. Truss the chicken *(see glossary for instructions)*. With your hands, massage the chicken with the oil and season with a touch of salt and pepper. Place the whole chicken over the mirepoix. Sear in the oven for 15 minutes. Turn the oven down to 350 degrees, baste the chicken with the marinade, and return to the oven. Repeat the process every 10 minutes for approximately one hour until the juices run clear and the chicken is fully cooked. Remove the chicken from the roasting pan and set aside on a carving board. The mirepoix remains in the pan to create the gravy. Place the roasting pan on medium heat and dust the contents of the pan with the flour. Combine and cook for two to three minutes, until the flour is browned for a nutty gravy. Slowly add the cold chicken stock and the whole rosemary sprigs and whisk to remove any lumps. Let simmer for 8-10 minutes on low heat. Strain the gravy in a fine colander and press the roasted mirepoix with the spatula or a wooden spoon to extract additional gravy. Add salt and pepper to taste if needed. Carve the chicken on a board into eighths and serve with the warm gravy.

Chef's Tip: If you do not have a roasting pan with a rack, you can cook the chicken directly on top of the mirepoix.

Chicken Milanese with Arugula Fennel Salad and Balsamic Reduction

Serves: 4

4 eggs

1 tbsp. + 1 tsp. salt

2 tsp. pepper

¼ cup water

2 tbsp. garlic powder

1 tbsp. + 1 tsp. onion powder

2½ cups panko breadcrumbs

2 tbsp. dry basil

1 tbsp. dry oregano

4, 6 to 8-oz. boneless and skinless whole chicken breasts, pounded to ¼" thickness (veal can be substituted)

¼ cup flour (for dredging)

½ cup extra light olive oil

Arugula Fennel Salad with Balsamic Reduction *(see page 106 for recipe)*

In a mixing bowl, mix eggs, salt, pepper, water, garlic powder, and onion powder. In a second mixing bowl mix the panko with the dried herbs. Dredge the chicken in the flour, dip in the egg mixture, and finish by dredging in the panko/herb mixture. Follow this method with all of the chicken pieces. Using the extra-light olive oil, pan fry the chicken in a 12-inch skillet over medium-heat until golden brown or cooked through, approximately two minutes on each side. Let cool and pat the chicken dry. Serve the chicken over a bed of Arugula Fennel Salad with Balsamic Reduction.

Stuffed Chicken Breast

Serves: 6

Special Equipment:
Plastic wrap

2 tbsp. extra-light olive oil
5 garlic cloves, minced
1½ cups shiitake mushrooms, thinly sliced
1 tsp. salt + 1 tsp. salt
½ cup pepperoni or salami, sliced thin and julienned
2 cups spinach, blanched (drain liquid by squeezing)
½ cup pickled cherry peppers, small dice
1½ cup pareve cream cheese
2 egg yolks
6, 6 to 8-oz. boneless, skinless chicken breasts,
    pounded to ⅛ inch thick
½ cup flour (for dredging)
4 eggs
2 cups breadcrumbs
Extra-light olive oil for frying

Preheat the oven to 350 degrees. In a sauté pan over medium heat, add the garlic and sweat until you can smell the aroma. Add the mushrooms and one teaspoon of salt and continue to sweat until the mushrooms soften. Cool to room temperature. In a large mixing bowl, combine the salami, shiitake mushrooms, spinach, cherry peppers, pareve cream cheese, two egg yolks, and one teaspoon of salt. Mix well. Line a cutting board with plastic wrap and place the chicken breast on top. Place half a cup of the mixture in the center bottom of each chicken breast. Fold the plastic wrap around the chicken breast and create a tight roll by sealing each end tightly like a candy wrapper. Place the chickens on a baking pan and let them rest in the refrigerator for 20 minutes to firm. Remove the chicken from the refrigerator and peel off the plastic wrap. Dredge each chicken roll in flour and loosely shake off any excess. Dip the dredged chicken in the eggs and lightly coat with the bread crumbs. In a medium-to-large sauté pan, heat the oil to 375 degrees; use a fry thermometer as hot oil can be very dangerous. Fry until golden brown on all sides for approximately 30 seconds. Finish the chicken in the oven for 25 minutes.

Porcini Burgers

When Daniel Boulud introduced his foie gras burger, he showed the world that a hamburger did not have to be a greasy, low cost, fast food item. He was my inspiration when creating this dish.

Yields: 4 burgers, 10-oz portions

Special Equipment:
 Coffee filter

2 cups dry porcini mushrooms
2 cups hot water
3 tbsp. shallots, minced
1 tbsp. garlic, minced
1 tbsp. extra-light olive oil
½ tbsp. salt
2 lb. ground beef (80/20 meat to fat ratio), room temperature
3 tbsp. porcini mushroom powder
Salt and pepper to taste
Porcini Aioli, *see page 195*

In a bowl, combine the dry porcini mushrooms and the hot water. Cover and let the mushrooms hydrate for 30 minutes. Strain and chop the mushrooms and reserve the liquid. In a sauté pan, sweat the shallots and garlic in the extra-light olive oil until soft and translucent and you can smell the garlic aroma. Add the chopped mushrooms and half a tablespoon of salt, and sauté for one to two minutes. Strain the reserved liquid through a coffee filter to remove any excess residue from the mushrooms. Add the liquid to the pan and bring to a simmer. Braise the mushrooms until the liquid dries. In a large mixing bowl, combine the ground beef, chopped mushrooms, and three tablespoons of porcini mushroom powder. Prepare a sheet pan with parchment paper, and with your hands form the burgers (don't over work them) and place them on the sheet pan. Let the burgers rest in the fridge for one to two hours to firm. Grill or bake the burger to desired temperature. Serve with traditional garnishes (lettuce and tomato) and Chef David's Porcini Aioli, found on page 195.

Brined Veal Chops with Peach Fritters and Apple Brandy Sauce

Serves: 4

Brine
2 quarts water
½ cup kosher salt
1 cup granulated sugar
2 bay leaves
1 bunch thyme
½ tsp. whole black peppercorns
1 whole star anise
8 cloves

Veal
4, 10-oz. veal chops
Peach Fritters *(see page 149 for recipe)*
Apple Brandy Sauce *(see page 193 for recipe)*
Pomegranate seeds for garnish (optional)

Brine

Combine all the ingredients in a saucepan and bring to a simmer for 15 minutes; let cool.

Veal

Clean and pat dry the veal chops. Lay the chops in a large, deep pan and pour the brine over to cover completely. Wrap the pan in plastic and soak for 3 to 5 hours in the refrigerator. Before removing the veal, preheat the oven to 350 degrees. Remove veal from the brine and pat dry well. Brown the veal on both sides for one to two minutes. Finish in the oven for 12-15 minutes for medium.

Garnish the veal with three to four Peach Fritters and spoon the Apple Brandy Sauce and pomegranate seeds on top of the veal.

Chef's Tip: This is a great dish for the holidays. Stone fruits are at their peak in the summer, but you can substitute pears or apples for the Jewish holidays or for Thanksgiving.

Mustard and Garlic Confit Crusted Fillet

Serves: 4

Special Equipment:
2 sheets parchment paper

4 tbsp. unsalted margarine
½ cup fine breadcrumbs
2 egg yolks
¼ cup Dijon mustard
1 tsp. cracked black peppercorns
20 pieces Garlic Confit *(see page 178 for recipe)*
4 fillets, approximately 8-oz. medallions (2" height, 3" length)
Salt and pepper to taste
4 tbsp. extra-light olive oil

Preheat the oven to 425 degrees. In a mixing bowl, combine the margarine, breadcrumbs, egg yolks, mustard, black peppercorns, and Garlic Confit (just 20 cloves). On a clean sheet pan, place one sheet of the parchment paper and cover with the mixture. Place the second parchment paper over the mixture. Role the mixture using a rolling pin to a $\frac{1}{16}$-inch thin layer. Place in the refrigerator for at least 30 minutes to set and firm. After removing the flat mixture from the refrigerator, gently place the four pieces of the fillets on the parchment paper. With a sharp knife, "sketch" the shape of the fillets and remove the cut-out shapes. Pat the filet dry and season with salt and pepper. On a lightly oiled grill or in a sauté pan, sear the fillets for two to three minutes on each side, until golden brown. Remove from the fire and set aside. With your hands, peel the top layer of cut-out shapes off the parchment paper and flip each onto the corresponding fillet. Bake the fillets in the oven for 12-15 minutes or until desired temperature is reached.

Moroccan Style Lamb Burger

Serves: 4
Yields: 4, 8-oz. burgers

1 tbsp. extra virgin olive oil

½ cup shallot, minced

2 tsp. turmeric

¼ tsp. cinnamon

½ tsp. cayenne pepper

¼ tsp. nutmeg

½ tsp. Spanish paprika

½ tsp. ground cardamom

½ tsp. cumin

½ tsp. all spice

1 tsp. onion powder

1½ tsp. garlic powder

1½ tsp. salt

2 lbs. ground lamb (ask your butcher for 30 percent neck and 70 percent shoulder meat at a medium grind)

In a heavy gauge sauté pan, add oil and sweat the shallots until translucent. Add all of the spices except for the salt and toast for 30 seconds until they smell fragrant. Remove from heat, add the salt, and let the mixture cool. In a large mixing bowl, combine the ground lamb with the spice mixture and divide into four, 8-oz. portions. In your hand, mold four individual patties and pack tightly. Let the burgers sit for one to two hours in the refrigerator to firm. On a lightly oiled, medium-heat grill, grill the burger on both sides for approximately four minutes for medium rare.

Chef's Tip: When combining the lamb and the spices, mix well, but gently, with your hands—that way the burger will not be too dense and the flavors will increase.

Coffee-Rubbed Flatiron Steak with Stuffed Baked Potato

This has been the Monday night special for many years at the Prime Grill.

Serves: 3-4

1 flatiron steak (approximately 2 lbs.)
Coffee Dry Rub *(see page 204 for recipe)*
Stuffed Baked Potato *(see page 157 for recipe)*

Pat the steak dry with a paper towel. In a mixing bowl, combine dry rub ingredients and the steak and season generously on all sides. Let the steak marinate in the dry rub at room temperature for half an hour. Grill the steak on a lightly oiled grill over medium heat for 6 minutes on each side (heat may need to be adjusted depending on the grill as sugar tends to burn easily). A black iron skillet or sauté pan can be substituted. Serve with a Stuffed Baked Potato.

Marinated Steak for Two with Fennel Puree

Serves: 2

½ tsp. all spice
¼ tsp. cinnamon
¼ tsp. cardamom
¼ tsp. nutmeg
2 tbsp. garlic, minced (4 cloves)
3 tbsp. shallots, minced (2 medium sized shallots)
1 tsp. sugar
1 tsp. salt
½ cup oil
32 oz. rib-eye, boneless
2 tbsp. oil (to sear)
Fennel Puree *(see page 148 for recipe)*

In a large bowl, combine all ingredients except for the steak and oil to sear. Marinate the steak in the mixture for 4 hours in the refrigerator. Turn over after two hours. Remove the steak from the marinade and sear on both sides for 30 seconds over medium-high heat in a non-stick pan. Finish the steak in a preheated 350 degree oven for 20 minutes (for medium-rare) and turn the steak halfway through cooking. Remove and let the steak rest for three to five minutes so that the juices can redistribute. To serve, slice the steak into quarter inch slices and accompany with the Fennel Puree.

Chef's Tip: *Always slice the steak against the grain to enhance the tenderness of the meat.*

Prime Grill Delmonico Steak with Peppercorn Sauce

Serves: 4

1½ cups panko breadcrumbs

3 tbsp. butcher black pepper

2 Delmonico steaks: ask the butcher for Delmonico
steaks from the shoulder of the ribeye, 20-
oz. weight, 2½ inches high, 4-4½ inches wide
each (This is what we do at Prime Grill, but we
recommend cutting each in half and serving for 4)

Salt and pepper to taste

¼ cup extra-light olive oil

Peppercorn Sauce *(see page 194 for recipe)*

Preheat the oven to 350 degrees. In a mixing bowl, combine the breadcrumbs and butcher black pepper. Pat the steak dry, season with salt and pepper, and dip into the breadcrumb mixture, pressing the mixture onto the steak. In a large skillet over medium-high heat add two tablespoons of oil and brown on all sides. Transfer the steak to the preheated oven and bake for 30-35 minutes for a medium rare steak. Let the steak rest for five minutes before serving. Serve the steak with the Peppercorn Sauce.

Pineapple and Lemon Grass Marinated Beef Ribs

Serves: 4

Special Equipment:
Zipper close bag

⅓ cup lemongrass (approximately 1 blade of lemongrass)

½ cup pineapple, small dice

3 tbsp. grated ginger

1 tsp. Chinese 5 spice

1 cup soy sauce

½ cup sushi seasoning

¼ cup lime juice

½ cup loosely packed brown sugar

20 pieces of cross cut 3-bone short ribs (ask your butcher for ¼" x 8")

Cut the lemongrass lengthwise and with the back of your knife firmly tap the lemongrass on a cutting board to bruise and extract all of the juices and fragrant oils. Finely chop the lemongrass

In a large mixing bowl, combine all of the ingredients except the short ribs and mix well. Add the ribs into the marinade and coat evenly. Transfer the ribs and marinade into a zipper close plastic bag and let the ribs marinate for one and a half hours in the refrigerator. Remove the ribs from the marinade and remove any excess particles from the ginger and lemongrass; pat the meat dry. The ribs can be grilled or baked. For grilling, lightly oil a medium-high heat grill and grill for two to three minutes on each side until desired temperature is reached. For baking, bake covered in a 375 degree oven for three to four minutes on each side.

Chef's Tip: There is a lot of sugar in this recipe, which tends to burn easily, so attend to your meat and adjust heat as necessary.

Helene's Holiday Brisket with Carrot and Onion Gravy

This dish originated from my mother, Helene. My grandmother, Bella, used to make a potted turkey dish with similar ingredients, which my mother later turned into a pot roast. It is perfect for the holidays.

Serves: 6-8

5 lb. brisket (ask your butcher for second cut brisket with the outer silver skin removed)
2-3 garlic cloves, thinly sliced (8-10 slices per clove)
8 carrots peeled, rough cut
3 onions peeled, rough cut
1½ cups marsala wine
2 quarts veal stock (chicken stock can be substituted)
Salt and pepper to taste
Sachet bag (1 bay leaf, 1 tsp. black peppercorns, 3 sprigs thyme, two pieces of clove)

Preheat the oven to 350 degrees. Pat the meat dry and, with a paring knife, pierce the meat and insert the slices of garlic inside each incision. Season the meat with salt and pepper. In a lightly oiled hot braising pan, sear the meat on both sides until brown. Remove the meat and set aside. In the same pot, with the natural oils from the meat, add the carrots and onions and caramelize over medium heat. Deglaze the mixture with the marsala wine and reduce by half. Add the veal stock and the sachet bag and bring to a simmer. Place the meat back into the pot and cook, covered, in the oven for two and a half to three hours or until fork tender. (Optional step: For the last half hour remove the cover and baste the meat every ten minutes to form a nice glaze or crust on the top of the meat.)

Remove the sachet bag and set the meat aside. Place the liquid from the pot, including the vegetables, into a blender and blend until smooth. Dress the meat on a nice large serving dish and serve.

BBQ Braised Short Ribs with Chef David's Signature BBQ Sauce

When I came to the Prime Grill this item was on the menu; however, it was being done as a red wine braised short rib. It was a good item, but it was very standard in the industry. I really wanted to offer my clientele a good BBQ dish, and short ribs seemed to be the best substitution, because of the long cooking time needed.

Serves: 4

2 lbs. boneless short rib meat
Salt and pepper to taste
2 tbsp. extra light olive oil
3 cups chicken stock
2 cups Chef David's Signature BBQ Sauce *(see page 188 for recipe)*

Preheat oven to 350 degrees. Pat the meat dry and season with salt and pepper. In a saucepot (or braising pan) over medium heat, heat two tablespoons of oil and sear the meat on each side for one minute. Add the remaining ingredients to the pot (disperse evenly) and bring to a simmer. Remove from the heat, cover, and place in the oven for two and a half to three hours or until fork tender. Turn the meat every 45 minutes. If the liquid starts to dry, add water. Spoon additional BBQ Sauce over the top and serve.

Mustard Crusted Rack of Lamb

Serves: 4

Special Equipment:
Brush

2, 8-bone racks of lamb
Salt and pepper to taste
2 tbsp. extra-light olive oil
½ cup Dijon mustard
2 tbsp. rosemary, chopped (stems removed)
2 tbsp. mint, chiffonade (stem removed)
½ cup breadcrumbs

Preheat the oven to 375 degrees. Pat the meat dry and season with salt and pepper on both sides. Heat two tablespoons of oil in a non-stick skillet over high heat and place the lamb, topside of the rack down, in the skillet and sear each side for two minutes. Remove from the heat, place on a roasting pan, and let cool for one minute. Wrap the bones with aluminum foil to prevent scorching in the oven. In a mixing bowl, combine the mustard and herbs. Using a brush, generously coat the top of the rack with the mustard mixture. Dredge the rack into the breadcrumbs on the topside only. Place in the oven and finish cooking for 15-17 minutes for medium rare meat. Remove from the oven and let the meat rest for three to five minutes before slicing.

Chef's Tip: Serve this dish with the potato shallot cake.

Side Dishes

Our marketing and public relations representative constantly emails me around the holidays asking for "something different." Finally, I came back to her around Chanukah time with two dishes that I am very proud of. A Quinoa Cake, which serves as a healthy alternative to potato latkes, and an Apricot Glazed Beignet, which features a classic inside-out twist to a jelly doughnut.

Creamed Spinach

Serves: 4-6

1 quart chicken stock
1½ lb. baby spinach, raw
½ stick unsalted margarine
1 cup onions, small dice
1 cup leek, small dice
2 tbsp. all purpose flour
¼ tsp. nutmeg
1 tsp. salt
White pepper to taste
¼ cup pareve cream cheese (regular cream cheese
    can be substituted if not serving meat)

In a small saucepot over high heat bring the chicken stock to a boil. Add the spinach, stirring constantly until all of the spinach is well wilted, approximately two minutes. Drain the spinach in a colander over a bowl, reserve the blanching liquids, and set aside. Using a wooden spoon, squeeze the spinach to remove as much moisture as possible, let the spinach cool, and coarsely chop. In a small saucepan over medium heat, melt the margarine and add the onions and leeks and sweat until soft and translucent. Add the flour and stir for two minutes creating a roux. Add one cup of the preserved blanching liquid and with a whisk, whip the mixture slowly, in intervals, whipping out the lumps for three to four minutes. Stir in the nutmeg, spinach, salt and pepper, and pareve cream cheese, stirring for another three to four minutes. Remove and serve.

Chef's Tip: Serve with the Flatiron Steak or the Garlic Crusted Filet.

Cauliflower Curry Puree

Serves: 4

1 cauliflower head, cut into florets (stems removed)

Curry liquid: 1½ tbsp. curry powder for each quart of water (see directions for measurement)

1½ cup leeks, finely chopped (only white part)

3 tbsp. garlic, minced

1 tbsp. ginger, grated

½ cup pareve cream cheese (regular cream cheese can be substituted if not serving meat)

2 tsp. salt

Place the cauliflower florets in a small heavy gauged saucepot and add enough curry liquid to cover the cauliflower (the amount of curry liquid will vary according to the size of the pot; therefore, prepare the needed amount according to the size of the pot you are using). Add the leeks, garlic, and ginger. Put the pot on high heat and bring to a boil. Reduce the heat and simmer for about 30 minutes until the cauliflower florets are soft. Remove from the heat, strain over a clean bowl, and reserve the liquids. Pour the cauliflower mixture into a food processor and add the cream cheese, salt, and ¼ cup of the reserved liquid. Puree until smooth and adjust seasoning as needed. Serve the cauliflower with teriyaki-glazed fish.

Chef's Tip: Use a bowl with a lid for the liquid. Don't add all of the water to the curry powder at once. First add a few tablespoons of water to the powder and create a "paste" then add the rest of the water slowly so that the powder will dissolve better in the water.

Sweet New Jersey Corn Flan with Sautéed Mushrooms

Serves: 6

Special Equipment:
6, 6-oz. soufflé ramekins

2 tbsp. extra-light olive oil
2 cups corn (fresh is preferred, but frozen can be used)
½ cup onion, minced
2 cups non dairy creamer (milk can be substituted for a dairy meal)
5 large eggs
1 tsp. salt
¼ tsp. ground white pepper
Cooking spray or vegetable oil
2 cups mushrooms, sliced (crimini or porcini)
3 tbsp. shallots, minced
¼ cup dry white wine (Pinot Grigio)
½ tbsp. tarragon, chopped
1 tsp. thyme
1 tsp. parsley, chopped

Preheat oven to 375 degrees. In a skillet, heat one tablespoon of oil over medium heat. Add the corn and onions, and sweat until soft and translucent. Let cool. Place corn and onion mixture into a blender and while blending drizzle in the non-dairy creamer. Blend until smooth. Add the eggs, salt, and pepper and continue blending until well mixed. Spray or grease the six soufflé ramekins and fill each ramekin with the flan mixture three-fourths to the top. Place ramekins into a two-inch-deep baking dish large enough to hold all in a single layer with some spaces between. Pour enough water into the baking dish to come halfway up the sides of the ramekins and bake for 25-30 minutes. Insert a toothpick or knife to check if the flan is ready; it should come out clean when the flan is done. Place one tablespoon of oil in a skillet and sauté the mushrooms and shallots over medium-high heat until the mushrooms start to caramelize. Remove from the heat, deglaze with white wine, and reduce until no liquid remains. Finish with tarragon, thyme, and parsley and season with salt and pepper. Slide a knife around the edges of the flan to loosen. Invert the flans, gently tapping to release. Spoon the mushrooms over the flan and serve.

Chef's Tip: The water bath prevents the eggs from curdling and allows the custard to cook evenly.

Fennel Puree

1 fennel bulb, core removed, finely diced

3 cups chicken stock (vegetable broth or water can be substituted)

1 tsp. kosher salt

¼ tsp. ground white pepper

¼ cup extra virgin olive oil

Combine the fennel, chicken stock, salt, and pepper in a heavy gauged saucepot over medium-high heat. Bring to a boil and immediately reduce heat to a simmer for about 45 minutes. Cook until there is only ¼ cup of liquid remaining (timing will change according to the heat and pot size). Pour fennel mixture into a blender and while blending slowly add extra virgin olive oil. Puree until the mixture is a silky consistency. Adjust the seasoning if necessary.

Peach Fritters

1 large egg
½ cup cold non dairy creamer
1½ tbsp. light brown sugar
¼ tsp. cinnamon
½ cup all purpose flour + ¼ cup for dredging
¼ tsp. baking powder
Vegetable oil to fry
2 ripe peaches (apples can be substituted)

In a mixing bowl, beat the egg with a whisk and stir in the creamer. In a separate bowl, combine all the dry ingredients. Stir the wet ingredients into the dry ingredients and mix out any lumps. In a small saucepot, add half an inch of vegetable oil and heat to 375 degrees. Remove the core from the peaches (skin can be left on or removed) and cut each peach into six or eight even pieces, depending on the size of the peach. Dredge the peaches in the ¼ cup dredging flour and dip the peach wedges into the batter until they are evenly coated. Fry until golden brown, approximately one to two minutes. When golden brown, remove and place on a clean towel to remove any excess grease. Garnish with a pinch of sugar.

Chef's Tip: For a dessert or a special holiday treat, dip in chocolate.

Potato Cake with Sweet Shallot Jam and Thyme

I am proud to be the chef of a world-class kosher establishment and always try to incorporate traditional Jewish recipes with my own twist. I knew my customers loved kugels, but I couldn't serve them a sheet tray of sweet noodle kugel. Here is my contemporary version of a traditional kugel.

Serves: 12

15 shallots, thinly sliced
1 cup balsamic vinegar
½ cup sugar
½ cup port wine
8 lb. Yukon gold potatoes, grated (approximately 12-14)
2½ tbsp. salt
¾ tsp. white pepper
1 bunch thyme (approximately 12-14 sprigs)
½ tsp. extra virgin olive oil

Preheat the oven to 350 degrees. In a heavy gauge pot, combine the shallots, balsamic vinegar, sugar, and port wine, bring to a simmer, and cook until dry. In a large bowl, combine the grated potatoes (remove excess water), salt, white pepper, thyme, and the extra virgin olive oil and mix until fully combined. In a greased baking pan (9x13), spread half of the potato mixture evenly. Pour the shallot jam on top and spread evenly. Finish with the remaining half of the potato mixture and cover completely. Place uncovered in the oven for approximately 90 minutes. Remove and let the cake rest for 15 minutes before slicing.

Wild Rice Salad

Serves: 4-6

4 cups cooked wild rice (prepare according to
    manufacturer instructions on the package)
10 tsp. white vinegar
10 tsp. extra virgin olive oil
½ cup sliced toasted almonds
¾ cup dried apricots, julienned

In a large mixing bowl, combine all of the ingredients and mix well.

Chef's Tip: For the best results combine all of the ingredients while the rice is still warm, which will allow the flavors to be absorbed by the rice better. Add homemade toasted raw almonds by cooking them in a 350 degree oven for 15 minutes. Pair this rice with our Mustard Crusted Rack of Lamb.

Quinoa Pilaf

Serves: 4

3 tbsp. shallots, minced

1 cup leeks, small dice (only the white part)

1½ tbsp. extra-light olive oil

2 garlic cloves, minced

1 cup quinoa, rinsed and dried

Salt to taste

2½ cups vegetable stock, hot

¾ cup cherry tomatoes, halved

½ cup olives, pitted and quartered

¼ cup basil leaves (10 leaves), chiffonade

In a heavy gauged pot over medium heat, sweat shallots and leeks in the oil until soft and translucent. Add the garlic and sweat until you can smell the aroma. Add the quinoa and toast while stirring for three to four minutes. Stir in one cup of the hot vegetable stock and let the quinoa absorb it while continually stirring. Add salt to taste. A wooden spoon or rubber spatula is recommended for this. After the stock has been cooked into the quinoa, continue by adding another cup of stock, and after that cup has been cooked into the quinoa, add the remaining half a cup and let the quinoa cook until dry. Stir continuously throughout the process. Remove from the heat and in a mixing bowl combine the cherry tomatoes, olives, basil leaves, and the warm quinoa.

Chef's Tip: You will know the quinoa is cooked when the quinoa start to spring open.

Quinoa Cakes "Latkes"

Serves: 10-12

2 tbsp. extra-light olive oil + oil for frying
¼ cup onion, small dice
⅔ cup quinoa
1⅓ cup water
1 tbsp. kosher salt + 1 pinch
¾ cup flour
1½ tsp. baking powder
1 egg
½ cup + 2 tbsp. soy milk
Salt to taste

In a heavy gauge saucepan, preferably stainless steel, warm two tablespoons of oil and sweat the onions until soft and translucent. Add the quinoa and stir for a few seconds to coat all the grains with the oil. Add the water and a pinch of salt and bring to a boil. Lower the heat and simmer until all of the liquid is absorbed. Remove from heat and let cool. In a dry mixing bowl combine the flour, baking powder, and one tablespoon of kosher salt and mix well. Add the egg and the soy milk and mix until all ingredients are fully combined. Add two cups of the cooked quinoa and mix. Heat two to three tablespoons of oil in a frying pan. When the oil is hot, spoon batter into mini pancakes (fist size) and fry for 30-60 seconds on each side, or until golden brown.

Variations

Fragrant Quinoa Cakes: Add 1 tablespoon of curry powder, ¼ teaspoon cinnamon, ½ teaspoon cumin, and ¼ teaspoon of cardamom powder to the batter mixture above.

Sweet Quinoa Cakes: Add your favorite dried fruits, such as toasted sliced almonds, toasted pine nuts, or dried cranberries, to the batter mixture.

Chef's Tip: It is always better to combine the dry ingredients first to prevent lumps.

Yucca Fries

Serves: 4

1 lb. yucca, peeled, julienned into matchsticks
1½ quarts extra-light olive oil, enough for frying
Salt and pepper to taste

In a small saucepot, add half-an-inch of vegetable oil and heat to 375 degrees. Rinse the cut yucca thoroughly in water. Pat dry and fry until golden brown, approximately three to five minutes, and until the bubbles stop coming to the surface. Using a kitchen skimmer or a slotted spoon, remove the yucca from the oil and place on a dry paper towel. Immediately season with salt and pepper to taste. Let the yucca fries cool and dry and save for later. Serve with Tuna Steak Frites.

Stuffed Baked Potato

Serves: 3-4

2 Idaho potatoes, thoroughly washed
1 tbsp. vegetable oil
Salt and pepper to taste
½ cup chopped crispy beef fry
½ cup chopped scallions
½ cup pareve sour cream
Egg wash

Preheat the oven to 375 degrees. Brush the potatoes with vegetable oil and season with salt and pepper. Wrap the potatoes in aluminum foil. Place the potatoes on a metal sheet tray and bake for 45 minutes to one hour or until fork tender. Let cool and cut in half widthwise. Scoop out the potatoes, leaving just enough potato around the sides to form an edible cup, and reserve the scooped-out potato. In a mixing bowl, combine the rest of the ingredients including the scooped-out potato and mix until smooth. Stuff the mixture back into the potato cups and brush the top with the egg wash. Bake until golden brown for approx 15-20 minutes.

Dessert

Desserts always start behind the eight ball at meat kosher restaurants because we lack a key ingredient—dairy! However, where there is a will, there is a way and we have created some inspiring dairy-free desserts that our customers have come to love. A favorite special is the pecan chocolate chip pie, which was inspired by two of our best customers: Ira and Barbara Lipman. I found myself cooking for Mr. and Mrs. Lipman and their family in their home. One day, Mr. Lipman brought me a pecan pie recipe from his wife, which I made and was in fact delicious. It had the perfect blend of Southern home goodness—a flavor profile that I love. In collaboration with Mrs. Lipman's recipe, I added my own personal touches, including adding chocolate chips to the recipe, and together we share this inspirational dish with you.

Vanilla Earl Grey Cream Éclair with Honey Glaze

Serves: 8

Special Equipment:
Pastry bag
Pastry brush
Parchment paper

Éclair
1 cup water
4 tbsp. unsalted margarine
½ tsp. salt
1 cup all purpose flour
4 large eggs + 1 large egg beaten and reserved

Éclair

Preheat the oven to 325 degrees. In a pot bring the water, margarine, and salt to a rolling boil. Add the flour all at once and stir with a wooden spoon until the dough forms a ball and pulls away from the sides of the pot. Remove from the stove and let cool for three minutes. Add the four eggs one at a time while stirring rapidly with the wooden spoon. Make sure each egg is fully incorporated before adding the next. The dough should resemble the consistency of mayonnaise.

Spoon the dough into a pastry bag, and on a sheet tray lined with parchment paper, pipe out éclairs about three-and-a-half inches long and one-inch wide or according to your size specification. Using a pastry brush, brush the reserved, beaten egg on top of the éclairs and bake for 20-25 minutes until golden brown in color and hollow inside. Don't open the oven while the éclairs are baking; it will impact the rising of the éclairs.

Chef's Tip: Paste the parchment paper to the tray with a small portion of the dough so that the parchment paper remains in place while baking.

Vanilla Earl Grey Cream

15 oz. pareve milk

1 earl grey tea bag

4½ egg yolks (approximately ⅓ cup + ½ tbsp.)

6 tbsp. cup granulated sugar

¼ cup all purpose flour

4 tbsp. cornstarch

1¼ tsp. pure vanilla extract

Honey Glaze

3 tbsp. cornstarch

4 tbsp. water

½ cup honey

½ cup roasted pistachio nuts, chopped

Vanilla Earl Grey Cream

In a small saucepan, warm the milk with the tea bag over low heat just before it boils. While the milk is warming, infuse the tea bag with the milk as if you were making tea. Meanwhile, in a mixing bowl whisk together the egg yolks, sugar, flour, and cornstarch until the mixture is completely smooth. Temper ⅓ of the milk slowly into the mixing bowl and whisk the mixture together. Add the remaining mixture back into the leftover milk. Continue stirring and heat it for one to two minutes, until the custard reaches 170 degrees on a digital thermometer and is very thick. Remove from the heat, stir in the vanilla extract, and chill. Place in a bowl in the fridge for one to two hours until chilled before filling pastry.

Honey Glaze

Make a slurry and in a heavy gauged saucepan, heat the honey until it starts to bubble on top (you will see how the viscosity changes). Add in the slurry and bring to a boil. Remove from the fire and cool to room temperature.

Assembly

To serve, fill a second pastry bag with the cream. Insert the tip of the pastry bag into one end of each éclair and fill.

Dip the top of each éclair into the glaze and let the excess drip off before turning over. Transfer to a wire rack and sprinkle the chopped pistachio nuts atop the éclair. Allow the glaze to set before serving.

Crème Caramel with Honeyed Apples

Serves: 6

Special Equipment:
6, 6-oz. ramekins

Crème Caramel
¾ cup sugar + ½ cup sugar
1 cup non-dairy creamer or milk
2 cups Rich's cream whipped topping (or other non-dairy whipped topping)
½ vanilla bean
3 egg yolks
2 whole eggs
Pinch of salt

Crème Caramel

Preheat the oven to 325 degrees. In a saucepan over medium-to-low heat, melt and caramelize half a cup of the sugar. Shake the pan occasionally to stir the sugar and evenly distribute the color. Caramelize the sugar till it has turned to a uniform light-tan color. Evenly divide the caramel between six ramekins. Swirl the caramel inside each ramekin to coat the sides and bottoms completely. Arrange the ramekins in a one-and-a-half-inch to two-inch deep baking pan. In a medium saucepan over medium heat, stir together the milk and cream just until it begins to scald, about five to seven minutes. Do not allow the liquid to simmer or boil at any time. Add vanilla bean, and remove the pan from the heat. In a separate bowl, whisk together half a cup of sugar and the eggs. Allow the sugar-egg mixture to rest for five minutes. Slowly add ⅔ cup of the hot cream mixture to the eggs, whisking constantly. While whisking, add the tempered eggs and cream back into the hot cream in the saucepan. Stir in the salt and strain the mixture through a fine colander. Carefully pour the hot cream mixture into the ramekins. Create a water bath in the pan holding the ramekins. Bake the custard for 35 to 45 minutes, until the custard is set. Remove from the oven and allow the ramekins to cool in the water bath for five minutes. Remove from the water bath and cool the custard at room temperature for 20 minutes, or overnight in the refrigerator.

Honeyed Apples

1 tsp. margarine

2 Fiji apples, peeled, cored, and cut into wedges

¼ cup honey

Honeyed Apples

Heat a non-stick skillet over medium-high heat. Add margarine and let it melt down, swirling it around the surface of the pan to spread the margarine and prevent it from burning. Add the apples to the margarine. With a wooden spoon, stir the apples around until they are completely coated and the margarine in the pan is no longer bubbling. Continue cooking until the apples are browned and slightly softened. Stir in the honey and remove from heat.

Assembly

To serve, run a thin knife around the edge of the crème caramel and invert onto a dessert plate, scraping any caramel from the ramekin onto the custard. Top with warm apples and honey.

Chef's Tip: Overcooking will remove the silky texture for which crème caramel is famous!

Chef's Tip: This is a great dish for Rosh Hashanah.

Baked Apple and Ginger Brown Betty

Serves: 6

Special Equipment:
6, 6-oz. soufflé ramekins

Streusel
⅜ cup all purpose flour
½ cup sugar
¼ tsp. ground cinnamon
⅛ tsp. ground nutmeg
1 pinch salt
¼ cup chilled margarine, medium dice

Baked Apple
2 tbsp. margarine
8 tbsp. sugar
1½ tbsp. all purpose flour
1 tsp. cinnamon
½ tsp. grated ginger
4 peeled and cored Fiji apples, small dice
Soy or pareve ice cream, opitional
Powdered sugar, for garnish

Streusel

In a bowl, combine the flour, sugar, ground cinnamon, ground nutmeg, and salt and mix well. Add the margarine and with your fingers sift the ingredients together to form small, loose clumps that resemble wet sand. Set aside.

Baked Apple

Preheat the oven to 350 degrees. Lightly grease the ramekins with the margarine. Coat the greased ramekins using four tablespoons of sugar and discard any excess sugar. In a bowl, combine four tablespoons of sugar, flour, cinnamon, ginger, and the apples and stir until combined. Evenly fill the six ramekins with the mixture. Spoon two to three tablespoons of the streusel on top of the apples. Bake for 30 minutes until the apples are cooked and the streusel has browned. Serve the dish with soy ice cream (vanilla ice cream, if serving dairy) or garnish with powdered sugar.

Chef's Tip: It is best to let the streusel mixture sit, uncovered, at room temperature over night.

Southern Pecan and Chocolate Chip Pie

Yields: 1, 9-inch pie

Special Equipment:
9-inch pie pan

Crust
1½ cups all purpose flour
1 pinch salt
8 tbsp. chilled margarine, small dice
4-5 tbsp. ice water

Pie Filling
1 cup raw toasted pecans, chopped
½ cup dark chocolate chips
½ stick margarine
1 cup sugar
1 cup dark corn syrup
3 eggs

For best results, prepare the dough by hand. In a bowl, sift the flour and the salt together. Using your fingers, crumble the margarine into the dry ingredients until it resembles yellow cornmeal. Slowly add the ice water a teaspoon at a time. Using a durable spoon, mix the dough until it forms a ball. Don't over mix: that will over work the gluten and the dough will become tough. Form the dough into a ball, wrap in plastic, and let sit for 30-40 minutes in the refrigerator. Grease the pan lightly and on a lightly floured surface, roll the dough with a rolling pin into a 12-inch circle about ⅛ inch thick. Transfer the dough to the pie pan and trim the edges.

In a mixing bowl combine all of the filling ingredients and pour into the unbaked pie shell. Bake in a preheated 350 degree oven for 55 minutes. Let the pie cool and set for three hours before slicing.

Chef's Tip: Work on parchment paper and before rolling the dough, form the ball into a thick disc shape; it will help you roll the dough into a perfect circle.

Chocolate Crepes with Strawberry Balsamic Gastrique

Serves: 12

Chocolate Crepes

1 cup flour

3 tbsp. cocoa powder

3 tbsp. sugar

Pinch of kosher salt

¾ cup soy milk (milk for a dairy recipe)

¾ cup water

2 eggs

2 tbsp. melted clarified margarine (butter for a dairy
   recipe or extra light olive oil)

Garnish

Non-dairy whip cream

Confectioners'/powdered sugar

Strawberry Balsamic Gastrique

1 cup *crème de cassis* liqueur

3 tbsp. balsamic vinegar

4 cups strawberries, cleaned and quartered

Chocolate Crepes

In a mixing bowl, sift together the flour, cocoa, sugar, and salt. Add the soy milk, water, eggs, and melted margarine/butter and whisk until smooth and fully incorporated—do not over mix. Cover and refrigerate for 45 minutes. Place a nonstick pan over medium heat and grease the pan; (cooking spray works well). Pour ¼ cup of the batter into the center of the pan and quickly tilt the pan in a circular manner so that the batter covers the pan evenly on all sides. The layer should be thin like a crepe. Cook the crepe for approximately 30-60 seconds, or until the crepe is slightly moist on top and golden underneath. The crepe will start to pull away from the edges and curl. Flip the crepe and cook on the opposite side for an additional 15 seconds. Remove and set aside. Repeat the process until the batter is complete. Achieving the perfect crepe can be difficult at first, but there is plenty of batter in the recipe for trial and error.

Strawberry Balsamic Gastrique

Place a small saucepan over medium heat and add the liqueur and balsamic vinegar. Reduce by three-fourths. The reduction should have the consistency of light syrup. Add the strawberries and warm in the gastrique to release some of the natural juices for approximately 30 seconds. Remove from the heat and let cool.

Assembly

There are a many ways to assemble this dish so express your creative side. Here are a few recommendations:

1. Blintz Style/Roll: Spoon the filling into the center of each crepe and roll the crepe. Garnish with the gastrique, fresh cut strawberries, whip cream, and powdered sugar.

2. French Classic: Spoon the filling on the top half of the crepe and fold the bottom half over. Fold again by half to create a triangle shape.

Chef's Tip: Sifting the dry ingredients is very important to achieve light and fluffy crepes

Molten Chocolate Cake

Serves: 5

Special Equipment:

5, 4-oz. soufflé ramekins

2 tbsp. margarine
1 tbsp. flour
8-oz. bittersweet chocolate, chopped
9 tbsp. margarine
2 whole eggs
4½ tbsp. sugar

Preheat the oven to 300 degrees. Lightly grease the ramekins using the 2 tbsp. margarine. Pour the flour into the greased ramekins and sift the flour to coat the ramekin. It is very important to remove extra flour from the ramekins to prevent white spots on the cake. Melt the chocolate and 9 tbsp. of margarine together over a water bath and stir gently until smooth. In an electric mixer, whip the eggs and sugar until light and fluffy or until the color changes from yellow to creamy white. Slowly stir the melted chocolate mixture into the eggs and mix well. Carefully spoon the batter into the prepared ramekins, filling each halfway. Bake in the oven for 15-20 minutes (the tops will have cracks, the sides will be set, but the centers will be very soft). Invert each mold onto a plate and let sit for about 10 seconds. Carefully lift the molds and serve immediately. Garnish with powdered sugar or cocoa powder.

Apricot-Glazed Beignets

Yields: 20 beignets

½ tsp. + pinch active dry yeast
⅓ cup + 2 tbsp. warm water
2 tbsp. sugar
¼ tsp. salt
2 tbsp. eggs, beaten
¼ cup non-dairy milk (milk if serving dairy)
1¾ cup flour
1 tbsp. melted margarine
Extra-light olive oil for frying
1 cup apricot preserves

In a bowl dissolve the yeast in the warm water with the sugar and salt and let sit for 10 minutes. In a separate bowl, combine the eggs and non-dairy milk and blend well. Add the egg mixture to the yeast mixture, add one cup of flour, and combine until smooth. Add the melted margarine and the remaining ¾ cup of flour and mix well. Cover and let the dough rest at room temperature for at least 30 minutes. On a lightly floured surface, roll out the dough to ⅛ inch thick and cut into 2½ inch squares. In a small saucepot, add half-an-inch of extra-light olive oil and heat to 375 degrees. Fry the beignets until lightly browned. Remove from the oil and let the beignets sit on a paper towel to drain any excess oil. Place the apricot preserves in a saucepan over low heat and heat until liquefied. Remove from the heat and dip the beignets into the apricot glaze. Let the beignets set, and serve!

Chef's Tip: These are a perfect substitution for jelly doughnuts for Chanukkah!

Cooking Foundations

The most important part of a recipe is beginning with a foundation that is concrete. Without a strong foundation, the recipe will fall apart. Some of the most important flavors found in a dish are created in the most basic cooking foundations that begin a dish.

Basic Vegetable Stock

Yields: 1½ Quarts

2 cups white onions, small dice

1 cup carrots, small dice

1 cup domestic white button mushrooms, thinly sliced

1 cup celery, small dice

2 quarts water

1 sprig thyme

1 bay leaf

1 tsp. crushed white peppercorns

In a small saucepot, sweat the onions, carrots, mushrooms, and celery until soft and translucent. Add the water, thyme, bay leaf, and crushed white peppercorns. Bring to a simmer and lower the heat for 30-40 minutes, until the mixture is reduced to one and a half quarts. Skim the impurities that rise to the top. Remove from the heat and strain. This stock can be reduced down to ¼ volume and placed into ice cube trays to freeze for later use. This is great to have in your home to add to sauces or soups as a last minute flavor booster.

Basic Chicken Stock

Yields: 2 - 2½ Quarts

8 lbs. chicken bones, skinless and rinsed
6 quarts water (cold or room temperature)
½ lb. onions, medium dice
¼ lb. carrot, medium dice
¼ lb. celery, leaves removed, medium dice
1 sprig thyme
1 bay leaf
10 crushed white peppercorns
2 garlic cloves
3 sprigs Italian parsley

Place the chicken bones in a stockpot and add the water. Bring to a boil and immediately reduce heat to bring the stock to a lazy bubble. Skim the foam and grease from the surface of the mixture and discard. Add the remaining ingredients and simmer, uncovered, for six hours, continually skimming off the foam and grease that rises to the surface. Remove the saucepot from the heat and strain the stock through a fine colander. Skim off any additional foam or grease. This stock can be reduced down to ¼ volume and placed into ice cube trays to freeze for later use. This is great to have in your home to add to sauces or soups as a last-minute flavor booster.

Chef's Tip: The key to this stock is to bring the mixture to a simmer immediately after boiling. Don't forget, a good stock is a clear stock! If the stock is not turned to a simmer immediately, the impurities that rise to the top will be boiled back into the stock, yielding a cloudy stock.

Basic Veal Stock

Yield: 3½ quarts

8 lbs. veal bones, cut in pieces by your butcher to
   extract more flavor and gelatin

2 gallons of water, cold

½ cup onions, medium dice (approximately 1 medium
   onion)

¼ cup carrots, medium dice (approximately 1 medium
   carrot)

¼ cup celery, medium dice (approximately 3 medium
   celery stalks, leaves removed)

1 sprig thyme

1 bay leaf

1 tsp. crushed white peppercorns

2 garlic cloves, smashed

2 whole parsley stems

½ cup tomato paste

In a stockpot over medium heat, place the veal bones and add the cold water. Bring to a boil and immediately reduce heat to a lazy bubble. Skim the foam that rises to the surface. Add the remaining ingredients and simmer, uncovered, for eight hours, occasionally skimming off the foam that comes to the surface. Remove from the heat, remove the bones, and strain the stock. If using the stock right away, skim off and discard any fat. If not, cool the stock completely, chill, and discard any solidified fat. This stock can be reduced down to ¼ volume and placed into ice cube trays to freeze for later use. This is great to have in your home to add to sauces or soups as a last minute flavor booster.

Basic Mayonnaise

Yields: 1 cup

1 large egg yolk
½ tsp. salt
1 tbsp. lemon juice
½ tsp. Dijon mustard
1 tsp. white vinegar
½ tsp. garlic powder
½ tsp. onion powder
¾ cup extra-light olive oil

Place all ingredients except for the oil into a food processor and slowly drizzle in the oil using the blade attachment to create an emulsification. Sample the mayonnaise and add more salt or lemon juice to taste. Cover tightly and refrigerate for up to five days. Stir before spreading.

Garlic Confit

50 garlic cloves
Extra-light olive oil

Cut off and discard the root ends of the garlic cloves. Place the cloves in a small heavy gauged saucepan over medium heat and add enough oil to cover them completely. The garlic should cook slowly with lazy bubbles rising to the surface. Cook the garlic until soft and lightly brown for about 30-40 minutes. Remove the saucepan from the heat and let cool.

Chef's Tip: Save the oil! This is a pure garlic oil that you can use in the future as a marinade or it can be used in salad dressings.

Dressings and Sauces

Some people might use a sauce or a dressing to cover up or bring to life certain flavors of a dish. Our dressings and sauces serve a purpose in all of the dishes we create in the restaurant and are not simply a garnish. It is important to always complement your dish and not complicate your dish.

Chef's Tip: Fresh-made dressings and sauces can last anywhere from 4-10 days when refrigerated.

The Prime Grill's Lemon Vinaigrette Dressing

Yields: 1-1½ Cups

2 tbsp. Dijon mustard
2 garlic cloves, minced
⅓ cup fresh lemon juice
1 tsp. cumin
⅔ cup extra virgin olive oil
½ tsp. kosher salt

In a blender, combine the mustard, garlic, lemon juice, and cumin. While blending, slowly drizzle in the olive oil. Add salt to taste and use immediately or keep refrigerated.

Chef's Tip: *Adding the oil slowly is very important for perfect emulsification; adding the oil too fast can "break" the vinaigrette.*

Mediterranean Dressing

Yields: 1 ¼ Cup

2 cups red wine, preferably Syrah or Cabernet

1 garlic clove, minced

1½ tsp. oregano

2 tbsp. Dijon mustard

1 tbsp. red wine vinegar

2 tsp. sugar

Salt and pepper to taste

1 cup extra-light olive oil

In a saucepot over a low flame, reduce 2 cups of red wine and garlic to ¼ cup, adding in the garlic in the last 20 seconds of the reduction. Once reduced, add the oregano and set aside to cool. Combine remaining ingredients except the oil in a blender and blend until smooth. Continue blending while adding the oil to create an emulsion.

Ranch Dressing

Yield: 1 quart

¾ cup raw beef fry, small dice

1 cup + 2 tbsp. extra-light olive oil

⅓ cup shallots, minced (approximately 2 medium
    shallots)

¼ cup jalapeno peppers, minced (approximately
    2 medium jalapeno peppers; keep in mind that
    jalapeno peppers' level of heat can vary from
    pepper to pepper, so adjust accordingly)

3 tbsp. garlic, minced (approximately 6 cloves)

¼ cup sugar

½ cup white vinegar

3 egg yolks

1 tbsp. garlic powder

¼ tbsp. cayenne pepper

2 tbsp. Dijon mustard

1 cup sun dried tomatoes, roughly chopped

¾ cup water

Salt and pepper to taste

In a sauté pan, place the beef fry in two tablespoons of extra-light olive oil and render out the beef fry (to make crispy). When the beef is nice and crispy, add the shallots and jalapeno and sweat until soft and translucent. Add the minced garlic, sugar, and vinegar and reduce by half (approximately 30-60 seconds). Remove from the heat and let cool. In a blender combine the egg yolks, the cooked shallots and jalapeno mixture, garlic powder, cayenne, and mustard. While the blender is running, slowly drizzle in the cup of extra-light olive oil. Add the sundried tomatoes, beef fry, and the water, and blend. Sprinkle salt and pepper to taste. Use immediately or keep refrigerated.

Chef's Tip: Adding the oil slowly is very important for a strong emulsification; adding the oil fast can "break" the vinaigrette.

Horseradish Dressing

Yields: 1½ cups

1½ tsp. Dijon mustard
2 egg yolks
3 tbsp. white horseradish
2 tsp. white vinegar
1 cup extra-light olive oil
2 tbsp. water
1 cup loosely packed fresh basil
Salt and white pepper to taste

In a blender, blend mustard, egg yolks, horseradish, and vinegar. In a steady stream, slowly add the oil while blending. Add in the water and basil and pulse. Finish with salt and white pepper to taste.

Horseradish Aioli

Yields: 1 cup

1 cup mayonnaise (use our Basic Mayonnaise, *page 177*, or any commercial mayonnaise)

2 tbsp. prepared white horseradish (strain excess liquid)

In a bowl, blend all the ingredients until evenly mixed. Over mixing can "break" the mayonnaise.

Chimichurri Dressing (Marinade)

Yields: 2 cups

1 cup cilantro, stems intact

1 tsp. Dijon mustard

1 jalapeno, deseeded (less if spicy)

2 garlic cloves

1 small shallot, rough cut

1 tbsp. lime juice

2 tbsp. red wine vinegar

Salt and black pepper to taste

1½ cups extra-light olive oil

1 tsp. cumin

In a blender, blend all of the ingredients except for the oil. While blending on a medium speed, slowly add in the oil.

Ginger Soy Glaze

Yields: 1 Cup

1 cup orange juice
¼ cup low sodium soy sauce
¼ cup + 1 tbsp. honey
1 tbsp. brown sugar
1 tbsp. fresh ginger, grated
½ an orange
1 tbsp. cornstarch
1 tbsp. water

In a small heavy gauge saucepot reduce the orange juice by half and add the soy sauce, honey, sugar, ginger, and the half orange and simmer slowly for 30 minutes. In a small mixing bowl, combine the cornstarch and water and create a slurry. Add the slurry to the pot and whisk until the mixture comes to a simmer and thickens. Remove from the heat and strain.

Chef's Tip: This glaze is perfect for fish.

Chef David's Signature BBQ Sauce

Although we know a good piece of meat only needs a little salt and pepper, what sets our restaurant apart are the signature items that we have created to enhance our delicate pieces of meat. My signature BBQ sauce is one my most proud dishes and an absolute favorite of our customers.

Yields: 3 cups

2 tbsp. extra-light olive oil
3 seedless jalapeno peppers, minced (check the heat
   of the peppers and adjust accordingly)
1 white onion, minced
1 tbsp. garlic, minced
¼ cup molasses
1 cup dark brown sugar
¾ cup red wine vinegar
1 cup coffee, brewed
1 tbsp. dry mustard
1 tsp. ground cumin
⅛ tsp. liquid smoke (optional)
2 cups ketchup
Salt and pepper to taste

In a lightly oiled heavy gauged saucepot over medium heat sweat the jalapenos, onion, and garlic until soft and translucent. In a mixing bowl combine the remaining ingredients, except for the ketchup, salt, and pepper. Add the mixture to the saucepot and slowly reduce by one-third. Add the ketchup and simmer for 1 hour on a low burner, stirring often. Let the mixture cool, place into a blender, and blend until smooth. Add salt and pepper to taste.

Chef's Tip: If using this product when grilling, be careful not to burn the meat because the sauce contains a lot of sugar.

THE PRIME GRILL COOKBOOK

Mango Coulis

Yields: 1½ cups

¼ cup red onion
1 cup peeled mango, cubed (add 1 tbsp. sugar if not ripe)
5 tbsp. extra-virgin olive oil
1 tbsp. lemon juice
¼ tsp. salt
⅛ tsp. liquid smoke (optional)

In a sauté pan cook the onions and mango in the oil until soft for approximately three to five minutes. Add the lemon juice, season with salt, and cook slowly on low heat for 10 minutes. Add liquid smoke if desired and puree the mixture in a blender until smooth.

Chef's Tip: Serve with the short rib empanadas or with any white delicate fish, for example snapper, halibut, or striped bass.

White Bean, Curry, and Basil Sauce

Yields: 2 cups

3 tbsp. extra-light olive oil
1 shallot, minced
1 garlic clove, minced
1 small seedless and ribless yellow pepper, small dice
1 cup cooked white beans
1 cup chicken stock
1½ tbsps. curry powder
¼ cup fresh mint leaves
½ cup fresh basil
Salt to taste
Pinch red pepper flakes (optional)

In a saucepot over medium heat cook the shallots, garlic, and yellow pepper in oil until soft and translucent. Add the white beans, stock, and curry powder and simmer for 15 minutes. Remove from heat, add the mint and basil, and puree in a blender to a velvet consistency. Season with salt and red pepper flakes.

Chef's Tip: Serve with the Lamb Meatballs. It also pairs well with Crispy Eggplant Spring Rolls or the Falafel Crusted Salmon.

Chef's Tip: It is important to release the steam when blending hot liquids by pulsing the blender a few times to avoid a dangerous mess.

Lemon Caper Olive Oil

Yields: ½ cup

⅓ cup scallions, thinly sliced (approximately
   2 scallions)
¼ cup rinsed capers
⅓ cup extra-virgin olive oil
1½ tbsp. fresh lemon juice (1 lemon)
Salt to taste

Combine all ingredients in a large mixing bowl and add salt to taste. Sauce can be served warm or cold.

Horseradish Zabaglione

Serves: 4

Special Equipment:
  Balloon whip

3 egg yolks
3 tbsp. champagne
1 tbsp. prepared white horseradish (strain excess
   liquid)
Salt and pepper to taste

Place a double boiler on the stove over high heat. Before heating, place all of the ingredients in a bowl and with a balloon whip (one that is flexible with fine wire) whip the mixture until it starts to aerate and create foam. Place the bowl on the double boiler and continue to whip vigorously so that the contents cook evenly. Cook this mixture until it thickens to resemble custard and is able to coat the back of a spoon. Cover with plastic wrap and keep warm until ready to serve.

Chef's Tip: Make sure not to boil or reheat the mixture, as the eggs will scramble. Please note that this sauce cannot be stored overnight in the refrigerator and reheated.

THE PRIME GRILL COOKBOOK

Apple Brandy Sauce

Yields: 1 cup

½ cup shallots, minced
1 tsp. vegetable oil
⅓ cup cognac
1 tbsp. sugar
1 cup apple schnapps
1 quart veal stock
3 tbsp. pomegranate seeds (optional)

In a heavy gauge saucepot, cook the shallots in the oil until soft and translucent. Deglaze with the cognac off the heat and keep off the heat for a minute to prevent flambé. Place back on the heat and reduce by half. Add the sugar and schnapps and reduce by half again. Add the veal stock and 2½ tbsp. pomegranate seeds, if desired, and let simmer. Reduce to ¾ cup or until mixture reaches sauce consistency and set aside. Garnish with the remaining pomegranate seeds.

Peppercorn Sauce

Yields: 1-2 Cups

3 tbsp. shallots, minced (1 medium shallot)
1 tbsp. oil
2 tsp. butcher ground black pepper
½ cup brandy
½ cup red wine
3 cups veal stock
5 tbsp. "cream cheese" (tofu cream cheese)
Salt to taste

In a saucepot sweat the shallots in the oil, until they become soft and translucent. Add the peppercorns and toast them until fragrant (one to two minutes). Carefully remove the pan from the heat and deglaze with the brandy away from any flames. When the fizzing stops, place over medium heat and reduce by half. Add the red wine and reduced by half again. Add the veal stock and reduce by three-fourths. Remove from the heat, and whisk in the "cream cheese" to finish the sauce. The sauce should be smooth and creamy. Add salt to taste.

Porcini Aioli

Serves 4

1 cup mayonnaise *(see page 177 for recipe)*
2 tsp. dried porcini powder
½ tsp. truffle oil

Combine all ingredients until fully incorporated.

Chef's Tip: *Serve with the Porcini Burgers (see page 127), steak fries, or with a baked potato.*

Tartar Sauce

Yields: 3½ cups

½ quart mayonnaise (use our Basic Mayonnaise
    recipe for excellent results or any commercial
    mayonnaise)
1 cup sweet green relish
½ cup mimosa of eggs
½ cup flat leaf Italian parsley, finely chopped
Salt and pepper to taste

In a mixing bowl whip all of the ingredients until fully combined. Add salt and pepper to taste.

Five-Herb Aioli

Yields: 1½ cups

2 quarts water (for blanching)
4½ tsp. salt
Ice (for refreshing)
1 cup tarragon, loosely packed, stems removed
1 bunch chives (approximately 15-20)
½ cup parsley leaves, loosely packed, stem removed
1 cup basil, loosely packed, stems removed
1 cup mint, loosely packed, stems removed
1 cup mayonnaise *(see page 177 for recipe or use any commercial mayonnaise)*
½ tsp. sesame oil
2 tbsp. water

In a heavy gauged saucepot, place 2 quarts water and 2½ teaspoons of salt and bring to a boil. In a large bowl, create an ice bath and put aside. Blanch all of the herbs in the boiling water for 10-15 seconds, and with a kitchen skimmer remove the herbs and place them into the ice bath for an additional 10-15 seconds. Remove the herbs from the ice bath and pat dry. In a blender, combine the mayonnaise, blanched herbs, sesame oil, and two tablespoons of water and blend until smooth. Adjust seasoning if needed.

Roasted-Red-Pepper Aioli

Yields: 1 cup

2 medium red peppers
2 tsp. extra-light olive oil
½ tbsp. salt
Pepper to taste
1 cup mayonnaise *(see page 177 for recipe or use any commercial mayonnaise)*

Preheat the oven to 400 degrees. Wash the peppers, pat dry, coat in the oil, and season with salt and pepper. Roast in the oven for approximately 20-25 minutes until the peppers soften and wrinkle.

Place into a covered bowl so that the peppers steam and loosen their skin. Once cooled, carefully peel the skin and discard. Pull or cut off the top of the pepper and gently remove the seeds and the ribs. In a blender, place the pepper with a spoonful of water and blend until smooth. Add the mayonnaise and continue blending until fully combined.

Chef's Tip: *Chop the peppers before placing in the blender.*

Roasted-Jalapeno-Pepper Aioli

Yields: 1 cup

1-2 large jalapeno peppers (according to the level of heat you desire)
2 tsp. extra-light olive oil
Pinch salt and pepper
1 cup mayonnaise (Basic Mayonnaise or any commercial mayonnaise)

Preheat the oven to 400 degrees. Wash the peppers and coat in the oil, season with salt and pepper, and roast them in the oven for approximately 15 minutes. The peppers will soften and wrinkle. Place into a covered bowl so that the peppers steam and loosen their skin. Once cooled, carefully peel the skin and discard. Pull or cut off the top of the pepper and gently remove the seeds and the ribs. In a blender, place the jalapeno with a spoonful of water and blend until smooth. Add the mayonnaise and continue blending until fully combined.

Chef's Tip: Serve with the Smoked Salmon Corn Fritters or pair with the Tuna Steak Frites.

Chef's Tip: Taste the jalapenos before they are incorporated into the aioli to learn the heat level of the pepper. All peppers vary in heat.

Rubs

Dry rubs are great because they can be made in advance
and stored in a cool dry space for many months.

Texas Dry Rub

Yields: 1 cup

4 tbsp. garlic powder
2 tbsp. onion powder
1 tsp. white pepper
4 tbsp. Spanish paprika
4 tsp. dried oregano
4 tsp. chili powder
½ tsp. cayenne pepper
2 tsp. sugar
2 tsp. kosher salt

In a mixing bowl combine all ingredients.

Chef's Tip: This dry rub is perfect for red meats and will last for up to one year in a cool and dry environment. For best results let the meat marinate in the seasoning for up to two hours before grilling.

Veal Dry Rub

Yields: ⅓ cup

1 tsp. cinnamon
1 tsp. ginger
¼ tsp. nutmeg
1½ tsp. ground red pepper flakes
1½ tbsp. fresh garlic powder
6 tbsp. ground porcini powder
2 tbsp. kosher salt
2 tbsp. sugar
1 tsp. all spice

In a mixing bowl combine all ingredients.

Chef's Tip: This dry rub is perfect for veal and other red meats. Store the rub for up to one year in a dry and cool pantry. For best results let the meat marinate in the seasoning for up to two hours before grilling.

Coffee Dry Rub

Yields: ¼ cup

¼ tsp. cayenne pepper
4 tsp. ground coffee
3 tsp. garlic powder
4 tsp. sugar
2 tsp. salt

In a mixing bowl combine all ingredients.

Chef's Tip: This dry rub is perfect for red meats and will last for up to one year in a cool and dry environment. For best results let the meat marinate in the seasoning for up to two hours before grilling.

Glossary and Terms

Aus Sec—French term meaning "until dry."

Blanch—To briefly cook in rapid boiling (salted) water and quickly cool. This process is primarily used for vegetables in order to soften, bring out the color, or change the texture.

Breaking—When an emulsified item separates.

Brine—Brine is a solution made with spice, sugar, and water used to season meats internally and to aid in a better yield after cooking.

Brunoise—Standard knife cut ⅛ inch by ⅛ inch by ⅛ inch.

Butcher Ground Black Pepper—Industry standard course ground black pepper.

Cheesecloth—Sterile gauze-like cloth that is traditionally used in the art of making cheese. In addition, cheesecloth can be used for straining sauces and making sachet bags to hold herbs and spices for sauces and stocks.

Chiffonade—Fine julienne of a leafy vegetable.

Colander—A bowl with small holes used to drain pastas or blanched items.

Confit—Translates as "to be cooked and preserved in its own fat." For example, a duck confit.

Coulis—A sauce that is cooked, pureed, strained, and cooled. Usually done with fruits.

Deglaze—Technique of adding a flavored liquid to lift up the fond or the foundation (natural caramelization/ proteins) of the food items that have been sautéed or seared from a hot pan.

Double Boiler—Also known as a *bain marie* is a stove-top tool that is used to slowly raise the temperature of a food item to allow for even cooking.

Egg Wash—One egg with a teaspoon of water used to brush breads and pastries to give a golden-brown sheen.

Emulsify—To incorporate two ingredients that would normally remain separate. We do this by adding heat, acidity, or agitation, or a combination of all three.

Flambé—This is the flame reaction that occurs when deglazing with a high alcohol liquid content. Remember to always flambé off the heat.

Hashgacha—Kosher symbol of supervision.

Heaping—A generous size portion or spoonful that is not leveled.

Julienne—Knife cut that resembles the dimensions of a thin matchstick.

Large Dice—Standard knife cut ¾ inch × ¾ inch × ¾ inch.

Liquid Smoke—Natural smoke concentrate that is used very sparsely to avoid the long process of "smoking."

Mandoline—A kitchen tool with different attachments that precisely cuts vegetables.

Mashgiach—Kosher supervisor or "Rabbi" who oversees the restaurant and kitchen and makes sure that the kitchen is maintaining its proper kosher standards.

Medium Dice—Standard knife cut ½ inch × ½ inch × ½ inch.

Mimosa of Eggs—Grated hard-boiled eggs (yolk and white combined). Often used to garnish caviar and smoked salmon.

Mince—To chop very finely.

Mirepoix—Traditional French culinary combination of onions, carrots, and celery.

Pareve—A kosher food term that means containing no meat or dairy.

Quenelle—Spoon technique used to portion out dumpling shapes or American-football shapes. To achieve, use two spoons that are the same size and with one spoon scoop a portion of the mixture and place the second spoon over the mixture and compress gently. Slide the mixture from the first spoon to the second spoon and place on the baking sheet, plate, or poaching liquid.

Render—To slowly cook a "fatty" item on low heat to remove the fat content.

Roux—A thickening agent used to thicken sauces and add flavor made with butter, margarine, or oil and flour.

Sachet Bag—Also known as a sachet d'epice is similar to a tea bag and is primarily used to infuse a sauce or stock with additional flavor. To create a sachet bag place the herbs in a cheesecloth, seal at the top, and submerge into a sauce or stock. When the desired flavor of the spices have been achieved, remove the sachet.

Sautee—To "jump start" high heat with a little bit of fat or oil in a pan. This is used to cook food items quickly in a short amount of time.

Scorch—When a thick soup or sauce settles while cooking and starts to burn on the bottom of the pan only. To prevent liquids from scorching, you must stir constantly while cooking.

Score—To partially slice with a knife, without cutting through the item.

Slurry Mixture—Most commonly a mixture of cornstarch and water that has a milky texture and color and is used to thicken sauces and soups.

Small Dice—Standard knife cut ¼ inch × ¼ inch × ¼ inch.

Sweat—To slowly cook. This primarily applies to vegetables in order to bring out the natural juices without imparting color and natural caramelization.

Temper—To slowly introduce heat from a hotter item to a cooler item in order to avoid curdling or breaking.

Truss the chicken—Method of tying a chicken to allow for even cooking and maintaining its uniform shape. In order to properly truss a chicken you need to follow five key steps. Begin by looping your kitchen twine around the neck (if there is no neck, keep it near the area where the neck would be) and bring the string upwards towards the wings and legs. Tuck the wings as you bring the string towards the legs; make sure they are tight against the body. Bring the string around and between the leg and breast and tie firmly. With the end of the string, tie the legs across the ankles and trim the remaining twine.

Water Bath—Technique used to slowly raise the temperature of a food item to allow for even cooking.

Index